CASE STUDIES IN

CULTURAL ANTHROPOLOGY

GENERAL EDITORS

George and Louise Spindler

STANFORD UNIVERSITY

SAN PEDRO, COLOMBIA

Small Town in a Developing Society

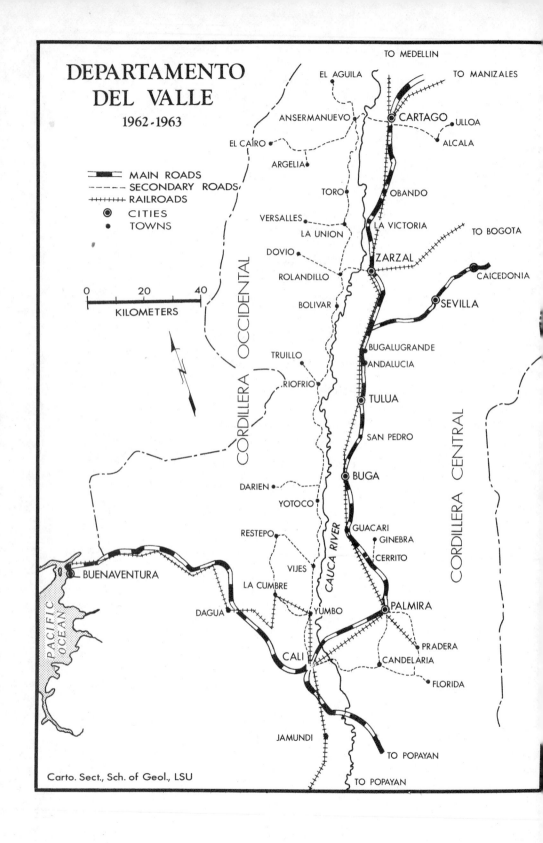

SAN PEDRO, COLOMBIA
Small Town in a Developing Society

By
MILES RICHARDSON

Louisiana State University

HOLT, RINEHART AND WINSTON

NEW YORK   CHICAGO   SAN FRANCISCO   ATLANTA

DALLAS   MONTREAL   TORONTO   LONDON   SYDNEY

To Valerie

Foreword

About the Series

These case studies in cultural anthropology are designed to bring to students, in beginning and intermediate courses in the social sciences, insights into the richness and complexity of human life as it is lived in different ways and in different places. They are written by men and women who have lived in the societies they write about and who are professionally trained as observers and interpreters of human behavior. The authors are also teachers, and in writing their books they have kept the students who will read them foremost in their minds. It is our belief that when an understanding of ways of life very different from one's own is gained, abstractions and generalizations about social structure, cultural values, subsistence techniques, and the other universal categories of human social behavior become meaningful.

About the Author

Miles Richardson was born in the small town of Palestine, Texas. At the end of his last year of eligibility as a high school football player he dropped out of school to join the United States Air Force. Four years later and armed with the Korean G.I. Bill of Rights, he began the process of getting an education. He received his doctorate in anthropology from Tulane University in 1965. In addition to work in Colombia, he has done field research in Costa Rica. He taught for two years at Indiana State University, and since 1965 he has been at Louisiana State University, where he is Associate Professor in Anthropology. He is a fellow of the American Anthropological Association and a member of several other societies. This is his first book.

About the Book

San Pedro is called backward (*atrasado*) by other Colombians; it is referred to as a "hole" by tourists; it is recognized as a very poor town by the inhabitants themselves. And yet its social life is comprised of normal, lively, interpersonal relationships. Professor Richardson makes the people real and their institutions understandable through the use of extensive accounts of specific behaviors of particular people as they engage in their daily routines.

The author stresses that San Pedro must be viewed as a segment of the larger society. It is the geographic basis of national institutions. Its political, social, economic, religious, and family patterns are specifically defined by Colombian society. Due to the poverty of the town, institutions and rituals are only faint replicas of those found in the city, however. The ineffective "bulls" in the bullfights and the town's church with its imitation brick front and broken neon cross contrast to their corresponding parts in the city after which they are modeled.

As social scientists studying small communities would generally agree, it is essential to understand the larger social forces which affect the community under observation. Professor Richardson provides the reader, in Chapter 1, with a sketch of Colombia, with maps of major geographic and political regions. Thus it is possible to place San Pedro in its social and cultural context and to get a glimpse of the forces that determine the quality of San Pedran life.

The author also includes in Chapter 1 an interesting discussion of the relationships between ethnic origins and social class. As is true of all Latin populated areas of the New World, Colombia does not practice racial discrimination—that is, prejudices are not legalized. The "ideal" type person is a White—defined as a person who reads, writes, and speaks Spanish and who does not work in the cane fields. The classification of Negro, Indian, or White is based on behavior, not biology. Thus an Indian becomes a "White" when he adopts the behavior patterns of the White. It is somewhat more difficult for a dark Negro. If he is educated and has an office job, he would be called a *moreno* (brown), which is merely a descriptive term with no racial connotation. The ruling "elite" form a separate class whose members have a respectable genealogy, a white skin, extensive land holdings and a university education. The group is flexible enough, however, to incorporate people with new, modern sources of wealth and power.

The important aspects of life in San Pedro—economic, political, religious, and familial are given relevance and meaning by using descriptions and reactions of the townspeople themselves. The reader learns, for example, the way *sanpedranos* feel about *cultura*, a most prized possession. *Cultura* means not only the material items but also the ideas of those possessing high status. It would include refrigerators, and so on, and the time and ability to enjoy poetry and literature. From the *sanpedranos* the reader also learns that the national government is to be scorned and criticized for its selfish exploitation. In viewing family life the behavior of eldest sons make it obvious that they have a deep, moral sense of responsibility for their mothers. And this is accompanied by strong emotional overtones. The reader also learns that many women today choose to enter into a "free union" relationship with a man rather than marriage. They fear being abandoned with no means of support if their husbands desert them. This is a very realistic fear in a community where divorce is impossible and where the earning power of women is extremely low.

While Catholicism is unquestioned, the reader learns that *sanpedranos* select the saints they wish to pray to and also select the particular commandments which they believe to be important, ignoring others. ("Love God," "Love your neighbor," "Do good work," and "Do not kill" are the most popular.) Dr. Richardson make it possible for the reader to experience vicariously events with the individuals involved. For example, during an Easter procession the reader finds out what actually ensued when the burro, carrying the figure of King Christ, refused to move. It is the understanding of these "details" of living that lead one to conclude with Dr. Richardson that in many important ways San Pedro is more like Hometown, U.S.A., than like an Indian or a peasant community.

Richardson's study makes a real contribution to methodology. He does not contrast his community or any aspect of it to the larger society. He suggests, instead, that we view San Pedro and comparable small communities as residential bases of national institutions.

GEORGE AND LOUISE SPINDLER
General Editors

Stanford, California
November 1969

Preface

The research upon which this case study is based began in January 1962 and ended in June 1963. The work was financed through a generous fellowship from the International Center for Medical Research and Training, Tulane University and Universidad del Valle. Partial relief from teaching duties in the spring semester of 1968 and a stipend during the summer of 1968 substantially contributed to the writing of this study, and for this valuable aid I am grateful to Dean Irwin A. Berg, College of Arts and Sciences, Louisiana State University, and to the Louisiana State University Research Council. I also thank Philip Larimore and his cartographic staff for preparing the several maps, Don Nugent for his assistance with the photographs, and Margie Pousson for typing the entire manuscript.

I again thank the people listed in my dissertation for their most helpful assistance, and in particular I am grateful to Dr. Forrest LaViolette for his warm interest and kindliness; to Dr. Thomas Schorr for not only sharing his experiences with me but also for his photographs of San Pedro; and to the people of San Pedro for allowing a neophyte anthropologist to live in their town. Anthropological fieldwork is the closest thing there is to rebirth, and for some of us the rebirth is painful. However, it is also rewarding, for as one struggles to be an anthropologist, he begins to wonder anew about his own identity and that of others. He gets a little closer to what it is to be human. For this experience I am grateful to the townspeople of San Pedro. I have tried to repay them by being honest, by not pitying them but by appreciating them, by not romanticizing them but by respecting them. The events and the people reported in this short work are real, to assure privacy, however, several names are fictitious and many persons are described as composites.

MILES RICHARDSON

Baton Rouge, Louisiana
November 1969

Contents

Introduction

COLOMBIANS PRIDE THEMSELVES on their bullfights. To validate their treasured Spanish heritage they demand that only the strongest of animals and the bravest of men face each other in periodic combat. Annually in Cali, as part of the December-January festivities, valiant men struggle for supremacy over fierce animals under the admiring eyes of the newly crowned queen of sugarcane.

The people of San Pedro, a small, poor town some two hours bus ride from Cali, also have their festive season, their beauty queen, and their bullfights. In March 1963, the local community improvement committee, the *junta comunal,* and interested organizations and individuals, planned three days of festivities to include the election of a local beauty, to be crowned queen of the chicken industry, and bullfights. For the bullfights, the interested parties had constructed a small stadium of split bamboo in the enclosed space just back of the *municipio* treasurer's office. Because they could neither afford fighting bulls nor kill the animals they did secure, the *sanpedranos* rented several young steers and a cow from a nearby rancher. Two teenage boys from a neighboring community had bullfighter's dress and so were hired as *toreros.* To advertise the occasion, posters depicting the traditional pose of a fighter gracefully side-stepping a charging bull were plastered on a few walls about town.

Preparations completed, the day of the fight arrived. After purchasing their tickets, the spectators cautiously mounted the rickety steps and gingerly sat down on the benches which immediately sagged a dangerous inch or two. Someone put fight music on a phonograph, and with the sounds of a *paso doble* blaring out, the two boys marched the few steps from the entrance to the center of the arena. While they were doffing their caps to the crowd, a young friend rushed out with his Brownie camera and took their picture. Then the "bulls" were let in. The first one, a young steer, despite his ears being split to make him vicious, charged only once or twice. Although the boys seemed content with the steer's performance, the audience was not, and two or three men lit newspapers and dropped the burning

1

paper on the steer's back. However, the steer refused to charge and was turned out, and the cow was let in. She immediately knocked one boy down and ran the other behind his bamboo barricade. This episode completely satisfied the boys' quest for valor and glory, and despite the abuse that the audience hurled at them, they refused to fight. Several men from the crowd impatiently jumped down into the ring and using their shirts as capes, provoked several rushes from the cow. She soon became exhausted, and although her slit ears were pulled, her tail twisted, and burning paper thrown on her, she could not gather strength to charge. So ended the bullfight; an ancient ritual that pits man against beast and in the process tears away man's pretensions and allows him to gaze upon his true self.

Perhaps one might expect a reaction, especially from aficionados, that this was not a real bullfight. On the contrary, as a bit of cultural data, the San Pedro fight is basic, and as is the case with all cultural data, it signifies.

What the fight signifies is that San Pedro is a poor, urban place, a small town, whose culture is that of the city but watered down, thinned out, and made sadly comic by poverty. Such a town does not have the colorful aboriginal rituals of some American communities, nor the quaint peasant notions of still others; instead its rituals and notions, bent by its small town environment, are those found in the great urban centers. The struggle of a group of people trying to act out the mighty drama of their nation on a minute, flimsy stage is so familiar as to be commonplace. Because the struggle is familiar and its pathos covered in platitudes, it is distinctly human; it is quietly heroic.

1

Colombia: A Brief Sketch

THE PEOPLE OF THE SMALL TOWN of San Pedro are Colombians; they are not abstractly average Colombians but are genuinely concrete Colombians. Other people, very different from those of San Pedro, have an equally real existence as Colombians. These people differ from each other and from the townspeople of San Pedro because of their geographic region, their ethnic group, and their position in the nation's class structure.

The Andean Core–the Geographic Heart of Colombia

On the political map of Colombia appear cities with a population of over 100,000. All except two, the Caribbean feeder ports of Cartagena and Barranquilla, are located in the Colombian Andes. The Andes extend up from Ecuador and at the Colombian border break into three main ranges: the Cordillera Oriental, which runs through the *departamentos* of Huila, Cundinamarca, Boyacá, the Santanders, and terminates at the Caribbean as the Guajira Peninsula; the Cordillera Central, which forms the variegated base of the *departamentos* of Tolima, Caldas, and much of Antioquia; and the Cordillera Occidental, which separates the upland Cauca River basin from the lowlands of the Pacific coast. Within the confines of these mountain ranges live most of the 17,500,000 people that populate Colombia.

The challenge of the Andes to Colombia's technological skills and economic fortitude, their varying climatic zones—where in a few miles the landscape changes from perpetual snow to luxuriant spring—and their aboriginal and colonial history have clustered people into distinct regions. Each region is commonly dominated by a single, rapidly growing city. Each region indulges in the pleasure of stereotyping itself and other regions: the peasants of Cundinamarca are fatalistic but cruel, the merchants of Antioquia always show a profit, the people of the Valle del Cauca know how to live the good life, and the aristocrats of Popayán fear nothing except a bad marriage. Each region, too, has traditionally displayed a measure of political

POLITICAL DIVISIONS

REPUBLIC
OF
COLOMBIA

CARIBBEAN SEA

Riohacha
Santa Marta
Barranquilla
GUAJIRA
ATLANTICO
Cartagena
MAGDALENA
PANAMA
Monteria
CORDOBA
BOLIVAR
NORTE DE
SANTANDER
Cucuta
VENEZUELA
CAUCA R.
MAGDALENA R.
ANTIOQUIA
SANTANDER
Bucaramanga
ca
Medellin
ARAUCA
PACIFIC OCEAN
Quibdo
CHOCO
CALDAS
Manizales
Tunja
Pio Carreño
Pereira
CUNDINA
MARCA
BOYACA
VICHADA
Armenia
Ibague
Bogota
VALLE
TOLIMA
Villavicencio
Cali
Palmira
META
CAUCA
Popayan
HUILA
NARINO
Florencia
VAUPES
Mitu
Pasto
Mocoa
CAQUETA
PUTUMAYO
EQUATOR
ECUADOR
BRASIL
AMAZONAS
PERU
AMAZON R.

National Boundary
Regional Political Divisions
• Regional Capitals
◉ Capital Cities Over 100,000
○ Other Cities Over 100,000

0   100   200

Carto. Sect., Geol. Dept., LSU

Leticia

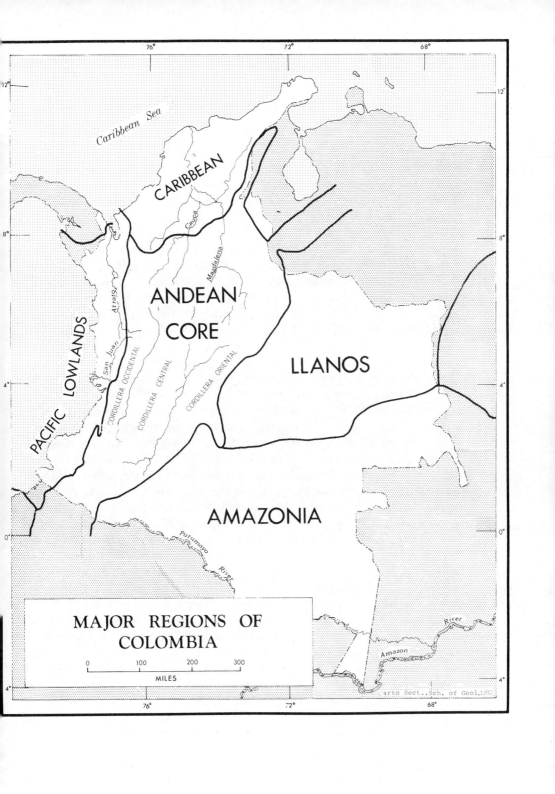

MAJOR REGIONS OF
COLOMBIA

Caribbean Sea

CARIBBEAN

PACIFIC LOWLANDS

ANDEAN

CORE

LLANOS

AMAZONIA

Cauca

Magdalena

Atrato

San Juan

CORDILLERA OCCIDENTAL

CORDILLERA CENTRAL

CORDILLERA ORIENTAL

Putumayo

River

Amazon

River

0   100   200   300

MILES

Carto Sect., Sch. of Geol., LSU

antagonism and jealousy toward the other areas and toward the national government (West 1962:3–21).

Chief among the Andean regions are the highland basins of Cundinamarca and Boyacá. Here in pre-Colombian times lived the Chibcha Indians whose level of cultural development and density of population were exceeded only by the civilizations of Peru and Mexico. Attracted both by Chibcha gold work and by Chibcha muscle power, the Spanish concentrated their colonizing energy in this area. One of the early settlements, Bogotá, soon became a political and cultural center of the colony of New Granada, and then as the chaos that followed the struggle for independence subsided, it became the capital of the new country of Colombia. Bogotá is still the residential base of the country's governmental apparatus and the home of its intellectuals. Colombians immodestly call their capital the "Athens of America" and to support the assertion point to the tastefully modern buildings that contain bookstores, art galleries, the nation's press and which adorn the spacious avenues crisscrossing the city. Interspersed among the office buildings are colonial churches that still testify to Colombia's Catholicity with their rich statuary of Christ suffering on the cross or lying dead in the lap of his mother. On the outskirts of the central complex of concrete and steel lies the not uniformly peaceful domain of *Ciudad Universitaria*. Here at the National University the colonial tradition of learning struggles to become applicable to the dirty problems of economic development.

Bogotá is truly an urban place and contains all the heterogeneity and contradictions that characterize any modern city. Former peasants, who have only themselves to offer at the limited market of jobs, flow into the city at a rate that is causing its proletarization (Torres Restrepo 1961). Workers, who have succeeded in the battle for low-paying jobs, may have to take on the traits of suspicion and jealousy that dominate the culture of the urban poor (Gutiérrez de Pineda 1958). Immaculately dressed career women, whose foreheads proudly bear the cross of ashes that the priest made early that Ash Wednesday morning, move briskly along the broad sidewalks (Cohen 1968). In the Congress and in the Presidential Palace the traditional elite fight each other over who will control the country, although they can no longer completely ignore the career woman, the worker, and the former peasant.

The altiplano peasants, whose sons and daughters swell the already full labor force in Bogotá, are both in culture and in race offsprings of the not always holy marriage of Colonial Spanish and Chibcha Indian. Hundreds of years after the union, the peasants continue to plow their small fields of potatoes, maize, and wheat with the old Mediterranean ard-plow tipped with iron and lacking a moldboard, and continue to speak in the syntax and diction of Cervantes. From their single roomed, straw roofed, dirt floored house, they view even their neighbors with suspicious reserve; yet paradoxically they are ready to fight for their identity as members of the elite controlled Liberal or Conservative political party (Fals-Borda 1955, 1957).

Only a few miles away, but centuries removed from the peasant's ard-plow and colonial idiom is the huge Paz del Rio steel complex. The plant, located near Sogamoso, Boyacá, draws on nearby reserves of iron ore, coal, and limestone. Along with the other plants in Bogotá, Medellín, and Cali, the Paz del Rio operation makes Colombia the sixth largest producer of steel in Latin America.

North from the Paz del Rio complex is another Andean region, that of the two *departamentos* of Santander and Norte de Santander. The early Spaniards all but ignored this area for it had neither gold nor a dense Indian population, and so European colonization took place slowly. Shortly after 1850 the white farmers began to plant coffee on their small mountain holdings, and with this new wealth the area, especially Santander, began to grow. The subsequent establishment of cacao, tobacco, and cotton plantations down the western slopes of the Cordillera Oriental toward the communication chain of the Magdalena River further stimulated development. An even more recent change in Santander's landscape is along the banks of the Magdalena. The government's autonomous oil company operates the nation's largest oil refinery at the river town of Barrancabermeja. In addition to producing chemicals for the nation's agriculture, the complex at Barrancabermeja is expanding into production of synthetic fibers to feed the textile mills of Medellín. As a product of these developments Bucaramanga, Santander's capital, has 230,000 people and is the second largest city in the Cordillera Oriental.

More distant from the cultural hearth of Bogotá, the *departamento* of Norte de Santander was colonized and developed at a slower rate than its southern namesake. The oil boom of Venezuela's Maracaibo Basin ramified into the *departamento*, and Cúcuta, its capital, has become an administrative center for the surrounding oil industry.

Due to the relative scarcity of a dense aboriginal population, the cultural adaptations that arose out of the struggles between the Spaniard and the Indian are correspondingly few in the Santander region. Conversely, the play of the New World experience upon the relatively pure European heritage has produced a unique familial culture. In the Santanders, the legally correct family, created when a couple marries in the Catholic church, is a family that the husband-father dominates not only in theory but in fact. The European concept of husband-father has developed to the point that the man is the economic, political, and intellectual director of his family. His wife is not the mistress of her house, rather she is a type of employee hired by her husband. By his command, she operates the house. Since, as local culture states, she does not have the capacity for intellectual development, she obviously cannot teach her male children. Her husband has this responsibility, and he grooms his eldest son to temporarily replace him when he is absent and to permanently direct the family, and the son's mother, when he dies (Gutiérrez de Pineda 1962).

Across the Magdalena River from Santander is a region that also lay in the backwaters of the turbulent days of Spanish colonization and a region whose participation in the coffee revolution in the last half of the nineteenth century brought great changes. Beyond these, the similarities between the Santander region and that of Antioquia stop. Unlike Santander the people who pulled Antioquia out of its stagnation were, and are, a triracial mixture of Europeans, Indians, and Negroes. These racial types amalgamated during the early colonial search for gold. The relative scarcity of gold and the cost of transporting it across the rugged

Antioquia landscape soon discouraged the large operator but stimulated the small, part time miner-farmer-herder. By the beginning of the nineteenth century and independence, the small farmer, growing maize and manioc, herding his black eared creole cattle, and augmenting his capital with small amounts of gold, found for himself a viable niche in the temperate zone of the Antioquia mountains. Perhaps because of the malaria-free mountain climate, his families were extremely large; a single couple frequently had as many as fifteen to twenty children. The children, as restless as their parents, pushed out of the hearth area of Medellín, settled the area that is now the *departamento* of Caldas, and were moving southward along both sides of the Cauca River when they encountered the coffee bean. They immediately began to plant coffee on the land they had previously cleared for their crops and cattle, and by the early twentieth century they were equaling the production of Santander. Today they produce more coffee than anyone in Colombia and more mild coffee than the giant country of Brazil.

The *antioqueño* drive to settle new land has not yet exhausted itself. The southern trust continues, and *antioqueños* walk the streets of San Pedro and other Valle towns. A great effort is underway to expand northward to the Caribbean sea, and for the first time *antioqueños* in numbers have moved out of the temperate mountain slopes into the humid, tropical rain forest of the Atrato River and the Gulf of Urabá (Parsons 1949, 1967).

The *antioqueños* do not restrict themselves to agriculture; they also build cities. A story is told of "a traveler who saw a large group of busy *antioqueños*. With the methodical swing of their machetes, they were expanding the margins of a raw, forest clearing. Curious, the traveler asked, 'What are you doing?' 'Founding a town,' they replied. Looking at the dense forest around him the traveler thought they were being ironic, but years later, when he passed through again, there was the town." (Quoted in Havens 1966:44).

The political map of Colombia shows how well they have succeeded in urbanizing their mountain vastness. The highest concentration of cities of over 100,000 is in *antioqueño* territory. The capital of Antioquia, Medellín, with nearly a million people, is second only to Bogotá. Manizales, Pereira, and Armenia grew under the impetus of *antioqueño* enterprise, as did to a lesser extent, the *departamento* capital of Tolima, Ibaqué.

This city building stems from the *antioqueño's* entrepreneural skills. The daring and vigor which he has applied these skills has placed him in control of many of the largest enterprises in Colombia. Of 110 concerns employing more than a 100 workers in the *departamentos* of Antioquia, Valle and Cundinamarca, *antioqueños* founded 68 percent (Hagen 1962:365). Much of this entrepreneural energy has gone into textile production, and Medellín, drawing both upon the traditional threads of cotton and wool and upon the latest of synthetic fibers, has become Colombia's textile center. Three of the big four of Colombia's textile plants are located in Medellín; the fourth is in the *antioqueño* inspired city of Manizales.

Out of these exploits in colonization, agriculture, and business there has arisen the *antioqueño* ethos. "In music, in poetry, in joke, and in folklore, the *antioqueño* is presented as the adventurer, the innovator, the astute man of business, the independent enterpriser." (Havens:47). Non-*antioqueño* Colombians attempt to shrug off *antioqueño* success. "Well, you know, they are *new* Christians," they explain and try to dissipate their jealousy by calling forth the *antioqueños'* supposedly Jewish ancestry. Regardless of his ancestry, the *antioqueño* stands as an uncompromising exception to the easy generalizations about Yankee ingenuity and the Protestant ethic of hard work. He is neither an Anglo-Saxon nor a Protestant—in fact he is the most Catholic person in an extremely Catholic country —and his entrepreneural adventures are as daring and as successful as those launched in Dallas, Chicago, or New York.

Southward from the Antioquia region and up the Cauca River the gap between the Cordillera Central and the Cordillera Occidental widens to form a long, narrow valley. The northern half of the valley is flat, and fields of sugarcane and herds of cattle dominate the rural landscape. The rapidly growing, boisterous city of Cali is the capital of the region's political division, the Departamento del Valle. Further southward, beyond the invisible *departamento* boundary, old, weathered volcanic deposits ruffle the valley surface. Sugarcane eventually disappears, cattle remain conspicuous, and the sedate city of Popayán administrates over the Departamento del Cauca.

These two regions differ in the ways that their capitals do: Cali, the raw, rebellious child, the third largest urban place in Colombia, a city which, between the census years of 1951 and 1964, doubled in size; Popayán, the colonial capital of an *intendencia* that stretched from Ecuador to the Caribbean, but now far down the list in size and in growth, a city which has "remained a colonial gem: aristocratic, cultured, refined and remote, like some elderly patrician lady who, cherishing the beauties of her youth, retains an aura of the elegant past undefiled by crass modernity" (Whiteford 1964:13).

The aristocrat of Popayán, whatever else he may be, is genuine. He is not some Johnny-come-lately whose wife scrambles through genealogies, looking for that one important link that will demonstrate the blueness of their blood. Nor is he the poverty-cursed scion who gallantly strives to repair the crumbling facade of his life. Instead, his lineage is impeccable; it goes back at least to the companions of the conquistador, Belalcázar, who founded Popayán in 1535. His wealth matches his lineage and comes from the true *caballero* source, cattle. His labors are correctly placed in the professions of medicine, law, and engineering. He serves—the unkind and partly blind say exploits—his country through active politicking, and sixteen of his fellow *payanese* have become presidents of Colombia.

He is proud of Popayán's artistic and literary tradition, the chief representative of which was Guillermo Valencia, whose *modernista* poems are nationally and internationally recognized. To maintain the vitality of the tradition, the aristocratic man writes poetry, literary reviews, historical articles, political polemics, and frequently teaches with honor at the local University of Cauca.

A true urbanite, he prefers to live in one of the ancient colonial houses that surround the central plaza. The house is a two storied structure, whose massive entranceway directly off the street often bears a coat of arms and opens into a gardened patio. Inside his wife commands a covey of maids and servants. Although she may no longer follow the practice of her mother and carry "at her waist a ring of keys which were doled out to the servants when anything was needed from the locked cupboards of the household" (Whiteford:86), she keeps a careful eye on the refrigerator.

The aristocrat honors his wife, but loves his mistress. Only the uncommon couple can reach across the barrier that inevitably separates the aristocratic male from the women of the same class. To seek those things that life prevents him from finding in his wife—intimate conversation and informal sexuality—the man may spend an occasional evening at his favorite house, or he may set up a separate arrangement for a mistress.

Completing the requirements of the true aristocrat, the man of Popayán supports the Church, and through its charities channels his type of concern for the poor. His social relations with the poor should approximate the standards set by the poet, Valencia. On the streets of Popayán, Valencia met a beggar playing a flute. The beggar, recognizing the great artist, "swept off his hat in a gesture of greeting. The maestro doffed his hat in return and, when asked why he had taken off his hat to a beggar, explained that the poor man had shown his good manners and in response, he [the maestro] could do no less than demonstrate that he was equally genteel" (Whiteford:208).

The last region of Colombia's Andean core is the Departamento del Nariño. In this *departamento*, which butts against Ecuador, the three cordilleras have intertwined to form a massive knot. Located in one of the small spaces between the mountain swirls is the region's urban center, Pasto.

Nariño and Pasto faintly recall Cundinamarca and Bogotá, as the rural population and much of the lower urban sector are mestizos. However, unlike Cundinamarca where the decapitation of the Chibcha nation fertilized the growth of Spanish colonization, the encounter between the Spanish and the Quechuas in this northern outpost of the Inca empire resulted only in an isolated, continual battle between the Spanish-creole hacienda and the Indian-mestizo pueblo. The juxtaposition of the large, privately owned hacienda and the small, communally owned pueblo brought forth a symbiosis riddled with conflict. The *hacendado* needed Indian labor to work his land; the Indian needed the minute amounts of money and goods that the work provided, but both the *hacendado* and the Indian needed the land that each occupied. The symbiotic conflict continued past independence, through the nineteenth century, and into the twentieth, when in the 1940s the Indians, now very mixed, opted for abolition of the communal holdings.

Conceived in the hostility between the *hacendado* and the Indian was a child ordained for despair. The child was the landless mestizo. Having adopted the language and values of the *hacendado*, the mestizo could not and would not rest in the uneasy comfort of an Indian pueblo; unable to accumulate even a fraction of the capital necessary to purchase life-supporting land, the rural mestizo took the only route opened to him. He became a tenant of the *hacendado*. Such a man in the 1960s is Asael Guachabés, worker on the hacienda, Bombona.

From the *hacendado* Asael receives about 7 acres of land. On this land he has built his shack and cultivates coffee, plantains, oranges, manioc, and a little tobacco. From Asael the *hacendado* receives 117 days of labor plus 25 pesos in cash (a little more than $2.50). The *hacendado* grades his workers according to their ability, and Asael was a first class worker. He had a serious accident and not only did he lose two years of work, but when he returned, his diminished productivity placed him in the second category. His debt to the *hacendado* for the use of the land, sharply increased by the two years lost, has reached the point that, at Asael's present capacity, he will have to work fifteen years simply to get even. If he is to get out of debt before he dies, his only hope is his eldest son. However, the son, having observed the luck of his father, is going to take his chances, risky as they are, with the city.

Asael ponders his fate, "I was born here, my parents and my grandparents lived here. What can we do? What will happen will be what God wants." But as he thinks of what God wants, he sings to himself this refrain, "Now my dogs are dead. Now only my lonely shack remains. Tomorrow I, myself, will die, so that it may be finished" (Fals-Borda 1964).

Be they tenant farmers, peasants, aristocrats, entrepreneurs, or urban workers, most Colombians live in the highland regions of the Andean core. The core protrudes out a lowland mass sectioned into the dry Caribbean, the rain-drenched Pacific coast, the primeval Amazon, and the grass and scrub-covered eastern plains. In the same way that it is geographically peripheral to the Andean ranges, the lowland area is socially marginal; its clusters of population are outliers of Colombian society, residues of old colonial attempts at colonization or new nuclei of people seeking relief from the crowded highlands. Yet because Colombia is a nation, and nations cannot live apart from each other, it strives to articulate itself to the world community through transportation pathways constructed across the lowland barrier, particularly where the lowland fronts the Caribbean.

The Caribbean

The colonial link across the Caribbean lowlands to the outside was the Magdalena River, and protecting this link as well as standing guard over the coast was the city-fort of Cartagena. Cartagena had one of the more successful histories in Spain's battle with the English privateers and pirates for control over the Caribbean, and today the highland tourist comes to inspect the 40-foot-thick walls that made it the best protected city in the colonial New World.

With the great need to get highland coffee out into the world market and to bring in the manufactured items that are still needed to supplement the increasing productivity of its own plants, Colombia could not remain satisfied with the Magdalena or with Cartagena. An increasingly efficient network of highways and railroads to move goods to and from the coast was constructed. To widen the bottle necks at the ports, the government has created the semiautonomous Colombian Ports Authority. With a 15 million dollar loan secured from the Inter-American Development Bank, the agency is expanding and modernizing the facilities not only at Cartagena and Barranquilla, but also at Santa Marta which, under the Ports Authority's guidance, may well become the principal Caribbean outlet.

Away from the modernizing ports and out into the countryside, a Negroid population works fields of tobacco and clusters around the still productive banana zone established by the United Fruit Company. Further from the coast the population becomes increasingly white. Among the sabanas of the Departamento del Bolívar, cowboys drive cattle away from the numerous rivers that spread out over the flat land during rainy season and then back to their greener valleys as the dry season returns. In the adjacent Departamento del Cordoba, *antioqueño* immigrants are making the Sinú valley a modern productive basin of rice, sugarcane, and cotton.

In their early marches across the Caribbean lowlands the Europeans pushed the aborigines either into the semidesert of the Guajira Peninsula or into the fastness of the Sierra Nevada de Santa Marta, located on the boundary between the Guajira and Magdalena *departamentos*. The Guajira Indians seem to have found a safe ecological zone for themselves, herding Old World goats, sheep, and cattle on land that more technologically encumbered Colombians find useless. The Indians of the Sierra Nevada de Santa Marta have to confront both the increasing penetration of mestizo farmers and the "mestization" of their own culture. The results are frequently similar to those which occurred in Aritama. In 1800 Aritama was an Indian village modified only by contact with traders and missionaries. By 1850 a mestizo peasant migration from the lowlands had penetrated into the surrounding valley and settled in Aritama. "The village became divided into an 'Indian' and a 'Spanish' *barrio*; subsistence agriculture was largely replaced with a cash-crop and livestock economy; religion-sanctioned monogamy changed into consensual concubinage and short-term unions. Color, class, and cultural differences became powerful status-defining factors. The struggle of prestige behavior increased individual and collective insecurity, and as higher formal control systems were lacking or unable to cope with the new situation, interpersonal hostilities spread and were openly expressed in malicious gossip and aggressive sorcery. This process has continued ever since" (Reichel-Dolmatoff 1961:xiii).

The Pacific Lowlands

The western stretch of lowlands that bounds the Andean core is the hot, humid, forested Pacific coast. As a geographic province the Pacific lowlands start in Panamá, take in much of the Departamento del Chocó, include portions of Valle, Cauca, and Nariño, and finally terminate in Ecuador. Although separated from the Caribbean only by a narrow isthmus and by the ancient, worn mountains of the Serranía de Baudó, its green landscape sharply contrast with that of the dry, brown Caribbean. The tremendous rains that fall on the Pacific area account for the difference. A yearly downpour in some spots of 400 inches makes the coast the wettest area in the New World. Responding to this annual deluge, the vegetation becomes gigantic and conquers the differences among flat land, hill, and mountain. "Seen from the air the canopy formed by the giant trees resembles a sea of green, overlapping umbrellas, broken only by streams and occasional clearings. Hundreds of rivers, often in flood, run through the forest from hill and mountain slope to the sea. They are pathways for human travel and their banks are the main sites of human habitation" (West 1957:3).

With the Caucasians fixated on the Andes, the two groups currently competing for riverine habitation sites are the Indians and the Negroes. As aboriginal as any Indian in the New World, the Chocó Indians spread themselves thinly along the rivers. They are not villagers. A settlement may often consist only of a single house, but under its conical shaped thatched roof may live several families. The Indians supplement their maize agriculture with hunting (done with a bow and arrow), fishing, and goods received from the Negroes in exchange for an infrequent pig. The two or three missions in the area have succeeded in baptizing many, but the Indians' ancestors still call to them in a way that Christ cannot. Most of the older men of one group, the Noanamá, can speak the vernacular Spanish of the Negro, but women are monolingual as are, contrary to expectations, the younger men.

The Indians watch Negroes coming up the rivers in increasing numbers and make an attempt at cordiality. Yet they cannot keep in check their suspicion and hostility toward these more successful people. Their attitude forbids them to marry Negroes—or the occasional Caucasian—and drives them to establish a new settlement further up the river or completely out of Colombia into neighboring Panamá (Reichel-Dolmatoff 1960; West:104).

The population that has successfully invaded the Pacific rain-forest are the descendants of African slaves that the Spanish brought to mine gold along the upper Atrato and San Juan rivers. Escaping or freed from the placer mining camps, the Negroes adapted the Indians' agriculture, changed the conical roofed aboriginal house into a four-shed, hipped one, and began to explore the West Africanlike environment in Indian canoes. Today they subsist on agriculture, and earn cash from their own small placer mines. They live in isolated huts or in a small line settlement where a church, a school, and one or two stores give the place sufficiently human character that sooner or later, someone names it. More recently Negroes have begun to reverse their dispersion into the countryside and are moving into the port of Buenaventura, immediately south of the San Juan River. Others have continued across the Cordillera Occidental and have descended into the Cauca valley to work on the sugarcane plantations or to look for jobs in Cali.

Buenaventura, although smaller in population than the Caribbean ports, handles more cargo. Its relatively early railroad link with Cali and the shortcut provided by the Panama Canal gave it an impetus that it is still enjoying. A sizeable portion of the Colombian Ports Authority loan from the Inter-American Development Bank is directed toward a further expansion in the port's docks, equipment, and warehouses. South of Buenaventura, near Ecuador, is the port of Tumaco, whose role as an exporter of lumber has expanded to include the importation of tons of equipment destined for the new Putumayo oil field in Colombia's Amazonia. The trans-Andean pipeline, now under construction, will flow oil from the Putumayo fields to the Tumaco terminal.

Amazonia and the Llanos

The discovery of oil in Putumayo is the latest of Colombia's attempts to exploit its vast eastern lowlands. This area is larger than all the rest of Colombia, yet it contains only half the population of a single Andean city, Cali. The political divisions express the lack of humans; only Meta has *departamento* status, the rest are either *intendencias* or the even less populated *comisarias*.

Nature has divided the area into two regions, the rain forest of the Amazonia, and the grass-scrub expansions of the Llanos. In the Amazonia, and apart from the Texaco engineers, Indian and mestizo agriculturalists move along the rivers. They trap mammals, birds, and reptiles to sell at the Amazon port of Leticia. Shipped out by air, these animals are doomed to be laboratory specimens or to decorate the zoos in Colombia and elsewhere.

The flat Llanos have been cattle country since colonial times. The *llanero*, like his counterpart in the much smaller sabanas of Bolivar, moves his cattle to the rhythm of the climate. In wet seasons, the numerous rivers coalesce to form shallow lakes, and the cattle and the *llanero* retreat to slightly higher land. With the end of the rain, the lakes return to being rivers, and the *llanero* spreads out his herds.

Presently, the Andean population is cautiously venturing down the eastern side of the core. In the northern corner of Arauca and Boyacá, missionaries are leading the way, as they did in colonial times. With the same goals as their fore-fathers, the missionaries plan to group the Indians in one spot so as to favor the transformation of migratory, pagan people into sedentary, Christian peasants, from people who live in the territory of Colombia into people who call themselves Colombians. In the same area mestizo-white farmers are percolating down the mountain sides. These are the unfortunates who not only lost out in the competition for scarce Andean land but who also were terrorized by the political upheavals of the late 40s and the banditry that followed (Stoddart and Trubshaw 1962). On the fringes of the Amazonia region in the Caquetá *intendencia*, peasants on their own and settlers with the backing of the Colombian land reform agency, INCORA, are attempting to make their mark on the tropical lowlands (Tinner-meier 1964). Ironically, the government sponsored farmers are producing no more than the independent ones, suggesting that INCORA is losing money—but it may be gaining the country a more precious commodity, nationalism.

The nationalization process has gone farthest in the least Colombian of all its regions, the tiny Caribbean islands of San Andrés and Providencia. Puritans from England landed here in 1629, but the first effective settlers were the English speaking, Protestant worshiping planters and slaves from Jamaica. Somewhere in the tortured history of Anglo-Hispanic struggles in the Caribbean, Colombia gained political control over these islands and then promptly forgot them. Recently her interest has reawakened, and through the declaration of San Andrés as a tax-free port, she has encouraged her elite to vacation on the island, making it a sort of subdued Colombian Riviera. The islanders are quick to gravitate toward this new source of income, and to more effectively care and feed tourists, many have become fluent in Spanish (Edwards, J., Personal Communication).

The regions of Colombia, their geographic base, their socioeconomic characteristics, and their cultural history, spread Colombians across the nation's territory and cluster them into semidiscrete units. The regions are only semi-discrete; they are not complete worlds in themselves, for at least in two ways Colombians of different regions resemble each other: the gross way of ethnicity and the finer, but still broad way of class.

Ethnic Groups and Social Class

Colombia, like its Venezuelan neighbor, falls in between the predominantly Negro Caribbean and the heavily Indian countries of Ecuador, Peru, and Bolivia. A substantial proportion of both racial types appear in its population, and these, mixed with Europeans, have produced an even larger array of mulattoes and mestizoes. A recent estimation of the country's racial composition is (Smith 1966):

Whites	25%	Mestizoes	42%
Negroes	8%	Mulattoes	20%
Indians	5%		

The Indians live along the socio-cultural fringes of Colombia, in the Sierra Nevada de Santa Marta, in the cordilleras of Nariño and Cauca, or in the lowlands of Guajira, Amazonia, and the Pacific. Although most Negroes and mulattoes similarly live on the nation's appendages, they, more than the Indians, have found space within the Colombian body—as their continual movement into the Cauca Valley testifies. The whites and the mestizoes constitute the country's Andean heart.

Colombia, again like Venezuela but also like all the Latin populated areas of the New World, does not practice racial discrimination. This is not to say that Colombians do not have a consciousness of race or that they are not racially prejudiced; they simply do not legalize their subjective feelings into laws.

Their race consciousness and prejudice is reflected in widespread comments. The logic of these comments are that there are three main races in Colombia: the Indian, the Negro, and the White. The Indians, the pure Indians, are not Colombians, but are backward people, savages still living in the Stone Age. The Negroes can stand up to tremendously hard work, yet they are frequently lazy, uneducated, and carefree. Because of their ability to endure physical stress, they are found principally in the hot areas working in sugarcane fields. The Whites include all people who have a minimum knowledge of reading and writing, who speak Spanish, and who do not work in cane fields. Whites are those that have *cultura*, "culture."

Humans and genes being what they are, racial features cut across the Colombian classification. The classification is based not on biology but on behavior. Thus, an Indian ceases to be an Indian when he gives up Indian ways, when he adopts a Spanish surname, speaks the Spanish language, wears European clothes, and does the things that White Colombians do. The case of the Negro is not as clear cut, because the behavioral classification does not completely override his dark skin. If a person of obvious Negro ancestry does not work in a sugarcane field, does not have the reputation of being lazy and carefree, and whose education permits him to have an office job, he will likely be a *moreno* (brown). *Moreno* becomes solely a descriptive term, which denotes the color of the skin, and its racial connotation falls away.

The Latin classification of Colombia is clearly superior to the Anglo classification of the United States for incorporating both the Indian and the Negro into the dominant group. Since it is primarily based on behavior, rather than on ancestral blood, the Colombian scheme permits people to change status within their own life time. For the Indian the change means going from being non-Colombian to being Colombian; for the Negro it means going from the twilight zone of barely Colombian to complete Colombian.

When the pure Indian and Negro change their behavior and become full Colombians, they move from out-class and semi-class to full class. They become parts of the highly visible Colombian class system. Although visible, the system is not easily comprehensible. Perhaps in no other area of Colombian life, unless it is in the causes of organized violence, do Colombian students lose their objectivity as in their comments about social class. The stereotypes of the class system, frequently expressed in scholarly literature, are nearly farcical: decadent, corpulent elite, having nothing better to do, ground the hapless masses under their cruel, Spanish heels. Responding, the masses seethe and plot revolution, egged on as always by the mysterious, well organized, hard core. The comments that follow may appear equally as biased; however, because they are based on the refreshing views of Robert Dix (1967: 42–63), hopefully they do not so vulgarly violate the realities of Colombian existence.

At the top of the three tiered system, and still guiding the nation's destiny as they have done since independence, are the elite. Unlike the other two classes, the elites of property, social standing, education, and of politics interact with each other and form not only a cultural category but also a social group motivated by a self-conscious tradition. The criteria for membership are a respectable genealogy, a white skin, extensive land holdings, and a university education. Membership is not closed; the elite do not form a caste. Some people fall out, others come in. This flexibility has allowed the elite to incorporate people with new, "modern" sources of wealth and power. The *antioqueño* industrialist, despite his tag of "new Christian," has become a member of the elite, his passage made ready through his careful maintenance of the elite-prized Hispanic virtues of Catholicism, kinship loyalty, and benevolent paternalism.

The middle sector is a category, not a group, of people who lack the proper combination of land, money, culture, and ancestry to be elite, and who do not usually work with their muscles. If their occupation—farming and shopkeeping—forces them into manual labor, they employ others to assist them. The middle sector differs from that of the United States in that the mammoth governmental agencies charged with the development of the country employ a greater percentage than do corresponding United States agencies. The Colombian middle sector differs also in the emphasis that they place on kinship loyalty, on the personal, paternal relation with lower echelon personnel or employees, and on their aesthetic contemplation of life. A final difference is that the Colombian middle class man exercises, perhaps, less control over the political process than does his North American counterpart.

Skin color darkens, education decreases, and sweat increases as one descends through the middle range into the lower sector. The lower category encompasses all those who lift, push, fetch, and carry in either the countryside or the city. The minute landowner, the tenant, the sharecropper, and the day laborer still outnumber their brothers in the cities. Their numbers are decreasing, but their aspirations are rising faster; they are more aggressive and more discontented than were their fathers. The urban division of the lower sector is headed by the permanently employed workers, whose efforts at unionization have brought them higher salaries, increased medical care, and earlier retirements. At the bottom are the sub-proletariats, the domestic servant, the shoe shine boy, the runner of errands, the beggar, the pimp, and the prostitute. No matter how miserable their life may be in a carton-board shack in the new slums that ring the cities, they feel better off than the rural laborers who periodically are lucky enough to work at the back breaking, and intensely boring, jobs of cutting sugarcane and picking cotton.

Both divisions of the lower sector, while their passions may not seethe and boil in the appropriate stereotyped manner, are increasingly aware of the gap between what they have and what they want. They, together with the people of the lower middle range, are threatening to the elite. In their response to the threatening appearance of the lower classes, the elite is attempting a difficult, perhaps impossible task. It is trying to reconcile the demands coming from the other classes with its own commitments. The elite is urging the country toward modernization, but in a manner suitable to elite self-preservation.

Colombian Modernization: An Elite Mission

The elite's oligarchic mission—to increase the country's economic productivity, to meet the most pressing needs of its people, to build a modern Colombia, and to still remain in power—is burdened by intra-elite competition. The Colombian elite is a single organization split into two complementary moieties. In a drama resembling that of the Republicans and Democrats but played more heroically, the two Colombian parties, the Conservatives and the Liberals, periodically act out the Battle of the Ballot.

Yet, the ritual encounter at the ballot box is not devoid of meaning. The two parties are ideologically opposed to each other at several critical points. The Conservative party sees itself as the repository of the traditional Hispanic virtues of Church, authority, and family. To call forth the ideal embodiment of these values, it refers to itself as the party of the peasant, for rural Colombia is where lasting virtues and social health are generated. To encourage rural development and because the party sees property as a natural right that the state must protect, it favors taxation on uncultivated land rather than parcelization of large estates. The Liberal party's mission is to free the individual from the stultifying effects of tradition and clerical domination; it is the party of the people. Its traditional posture favoring the lifting of all governmental restrictions on trade and consequently the decentralization of government has changed to one calling for the central government to take on a greater role in meeting the individual's social and economic needs. Holding that property carries with it a social responsibility, the Liberal stance is that if a landowner fails to meet his responsibilities, his land should be parcelled and distributed to those in greater need. Papal encyclicals are not the party's spiritual guides, but rather it lays claim to the thoughts of modern liberalism (Dix:231–237).

Following a period of retrenchment from the first massive efforts at modernization by the Liberal president, Alfonso Lopez, intra-elite squabbles grew in sharpness as the two parties jockeyed about in the early 1940s. While the elite were maneuvering in search of this or that advantage, the non-elite were listening to the messianic speeches of Jorge Gaitán.

Gaitán was, and perhaps still is, a unique man in Colombian politics. A man of ordinary ancestry but possessing a university education, he had climbed to the top of the Liberal party machinery. In this he was not particularly unique, but what made him so was his refusal to behave like an elite; instead, he went through the streets of Bogotá preaching the democratization and the moral restoration of Colombia. The crowds gathered and roared their approval on his ultimate proclamation: "I am not a man, I am a people." On April 9, 1948, an assassin shot him. Chaos exploded in Bogotá, and the turmoil of destruction killed several thousand people. For the first time, the tragic strains and inevitable contradictions of a modernizing New World society ran amok on the streets of a Colombian city.

The elite, or at least a proportion of it, reacted to the *bogotazo* by first supporting the hard fisted rule of the ultra-Conservative, Laureano Gómez. The man, who proclaimed, "Spain, marching forward as the sole defender of Christian civilization, leads the Western nations in the reconstruction of the empire of *Hispanidad,* and we inscribe our names in the roster of its phalanxes with inutterable satisfaction" (quoted in Dix:109), could not remold Colombia into the shape of Franco's Spain. Intrigue within his own party, persecution of the Liberals, and the formation of marauding groups in the countryside brought the impeccable aristocrat down. Control of the country passed from the hands of the elite to those of General Rojas Pinilla.

Perhaps at first a child of the elite, Rojas became an adult dictator. Following an initial period of creative energy, the Rojas government crystallized into a pathetic effort to become another Argentina, with Rojas as Perón and his daughter as Eva. With the country seemingly well on the road to economic, political, and social disaster, the elite arose to the occasion. Party leaders, the urbane Alberto Lleras and the stern Laureano Gómez, concerned with their country's welfare, met in Spain to solidify an agreement of cooperation. After attaching modifications to the agreement, the elite sought, for the first time, popular approval of their actions and called for a plebiscite. Although wags, including Rojas, scorned the plebiscite, saying that the peasants thought they were voting for *Don Plebiscito,* Colombians in December 1957 overwhelmingly approved the elite-constructed measure.

The agreement was that the two parties, united at the top into a National Front, would support a single presidential candidate until 1974. The candidate of the National Front would be chosen in alternate four year terms from only the two parties. All other elected positions and most appointed ones would be distributed on a parity basis between the Liberals and the Conservatives.

After additional maneuvering, the parties finally decided to offer the Liberal, Alberto Lleras, as their first candidate, and in 1958 he took office. Four years later, despite friction within each party and the emergence of new parties, such as the one lead by the surprisingly durable Rojas, power changed peacefully with the election of the Conservative, Guillermo León Valencia of Popayán. After another four years, one half of the sixteen year pact, the election of the Liberal,

Carlos Lleras Restrepo of Bogotá, continued the National Front. In his inauguration speech of August 1966, President Lleras said it was the will of the people that he should strive quickly toward achieving an accelerated development in production and a more equitable distribution of income.

As did the programs of his elite predecessors, President Carlos Lleras' program confronts the problems of transforming Colombia from being an economic hinterland of the United States and of Europe into a country of primary development, from an agrarian appendage of Western civilization to a New World cultural hearth. The task is enormous. Agriculture has to diversify to allow Colombia to escape the fluctuations of the world coffee market; agricultural productivity has to increase faster than does the population to prevent malnourishment. The inclines of the Andes either have to be smoothed out or flown over to get exports out and imports in. Scarce capital has to accrue, and capitalists have to invest in the high risk, native industrial plants. The nation has to change its social composition. The Indian, the Negro, and the poor mestizo and mulatto have to see their work as contributing to the country's destiny; resources—land, food, health, housing, and education—have to flow to them so that their presence is an honor to themselves and to Colombia.

Through the creation of semiautonomous agencies such as the Industrial Development Institute, which is encouraging further expansion of the Paz del Rio steel complex; the Colombian Petroleum Company, which operates the refinery in Santander; the Ports Authority, which taps the money of the richer nations for expansion of the nation's export-import capacity; the Institute for Agrarian Reform, which is trying to meet the thirst for land through parcelization and colonization; the Agrarian Bank, which makes credit available to peasants; and the Community Action Committee agency, which encourages local programs of community development, the Colombian government, under elite control, is attempting the transformation from hinterland to hearth.

Until now, those who have controlled Colombia since independence have achieved their goals of preventing revolution. They have remained in power and are modernizing the country. Yet their very success may bring them down. The thrusts of the elite's own programs and of processes that no man, no matter his qualifications, can control have produced a country greatly different than when the beggar and poet bowed to each other in the streets of Popayán. Today, "in public eating places . . . customers are likely to reprimand waiters or waitresses loudly and unmercifully for the slightest mistake. . . . Taxi drivers scold fares who do not carry small change, and bus drivers, belabored for their slowness, rudeness, or bad driving, may take revenge by deliberately shutting the doors on passengers as they try to get off the bus" (Erasmus 1961:83).

It is in this country, one of regionalism, of fatalistic backwardness, of daring entrepreneurship, of lingering aristocracy, of vigorous modernization; of cultural refinement, social barbarity, and intense suspicion that the people of San Pedro live.

2

San Pedro Town

HUMAN BEINGS, including anthropologists, approach each other with pre-conceived notions of what the other person, the stranger, is going to do and say. When these vaguely formed images are dug out of the sub-conscious and purified of their platitudes, they become useful models for cataloging the multitudinous impressions that radiate out of a new person or a new people. What model best catalogs the people of San Pedro? Are they and the place they live in more like the dispersed settlements of the Andean peasants than like the riverine houses of the Chocó Indian or Negro? Do they resemble the richly con-tradictory urban complex of Bogotá more than the smoothly traditional city of Popayán? Or do they look like and act like the people of Mainstreet—Hometown, U.S.A.?

For those accustomed to seeing only two types of Spanish Americans, the peasant and the aristocrat, San Pedro is a surprise. San Pedro functions, and *sanpedranos* act, like Mainstreet and Mainstreeters. San Pedro is neither a quaint peasant community, nor a glittering urban complex; it is simply a town, and its people, ordinary townsmen.

As a place, San Pedro is the political, educational, medical, religious, recreational, and to a diminishing degree, the market center of the rural area surrounding it. The location of these activities within San Pedro makes it struc-turally more complex than a hamlet or a village. The smallness in scale of these enterprises and the informality in which they are carried out separates San Pedro from a city. In the sense that it is neither village nor city, San Pedro resembles the North American rural town. Furthermore, just as rural towns in the United States are losing economic control of their clientele, so the merchants of San Pedro are hard pressed to meet the cheaper prices and larger ranges of goods available in city stores.

As a people, the citizens of San Pedro are not cultural isolates. They are neither primitive Indian nor archaic peasant; they are structurally, culturally, and psychologically Colombians. They are Colombians in the same quality that Main-

Street activity in the late afternoon.

streeters are North Americans. The bullfight of San Pedro corresponds to the super-bowl of Mainstreet; their Chicken Queen, although more beautiful in her naiveté, is sister to Mainstreet's Cheese Queen, Dogwood Queen, or Pecan Queen.

Mainstreet and San Pedro both proudly proclaim that life in a small town is better than that in the city. Both occasionally stop to wonder at the meanness of their small town worlds, but after a minute of reflection, both shrug their shoulders with soul restoring comments. The Mainstreeter says, "Everybody knows your business in a small town;" the *sanpedrano* makes a more terse summary: *"Pueblo pequeño, infierno grande"* (Small town, large hell).

Cauca Valley Settlements

San Pedro wears a town dress because of its position in the regional network of settlements and transportation lines that mark the Cauca Valley landscape. Dominating the settlements is the urban complex of Cali and its satellite, Yumbo. The third largest city in Colombia, Cali is the administrative, economic, and cultural center of the region. Nearby Palmira follows Cali in both size and rate of growth. Still smaller settlements are the provincial cities. Two such cities, Buga and Tuluá, surround San Pedro. Buga is a smaller, incomplete version of Popayán. The local landed gentry reside there, at least one colonial church still manages to stick its steeple through the tangle of light and telephone lines, and the city's ornate basilica houses the ancient cult of Our Lord of Miracles. In contrast, Tuluá, in its raw newness and commercial thrust, is more like Cali.

Interspersed among the cities and quite common on the more isolated left bank of the Cauca River are the towns. Proximity to cities—a proximity engendered and increasingly tightened by broader highways and more frequent bus service—makes towns dependent on cities. Townspeople go to cities for a greater range of goods, larger markets, a complete high-school education, a higher level of medical care, and more titillating amusements. Towns are the urban hinterlands of cities.

Be they city or town, each of the settlements appearing on the Departamento del Valle map are administrative units, *cabeceras*, of a land area that often extends from the river to the mountains. The area is the *municipio* of the *cabecera* and contains settlements that are almost always smaller than the *cabecera*. In places these settlements are nucleated into population clusters the size of which ranges from three or four houses containing relatives, to fifty or so structures. The larger clusters have two or three small stores, a minute school, a police station, and a chapel, which is periodically visited by the *cabecera* priest. Nonnucleated settlements in the *municipio* are the *hacienda* complex of the large landowner or the isolated shack of the small farmer or sharecropper.

San Pedro is one of the smaller *cabeceras* and *municipios* of the Valle. Its administrative leader, the *alcalde*, operates in an architectural and social setting that contrasts in intimacy and informality with that which surrounds the *alcalde* of a city, say Palmira.

To see the Palmira *alcalde*, who in 1962–1963 was an extremely pleasant, informative man, the interested person climbs to the second story of an imposing structure. On the second level he enters a large room occupied with clattering machines and busy people. He leans over the wall that separates the waiting area from the work area and asks the receptionist if he may see the *alcalde*. She looks up from gently tapping her electric typewriter and in a voice that matches her immaculate appearance, she says that she will inquire. As the person sits down under a time clock that records who comes to work and when, he notices that the office of the *alcalde's* assistant bears the sign, "Do Not Enter Without Being Announced." The receptionist returns and informs him that the *alcalde* is free. Once inside the office, the person shakes hands with the *alcalde*, and they both sit down at a long, highly polished table that separates the *alcalde's* desk from the office entrance.

To see the San Pedro *alcalde*, who in 1962–1963 was equally as pleasant and informative, the interested person steps from the street into the office of the *alcalde's* assistant. The assistant is seated at a scarred desk banging away at a manual typewriter. He hitches up his slacks over his sport shirt as he rises to check on the *alcalde*. There are no time clocks and no forbidding signs hanging on the chipped, adobe walls; the *alcalde* and the assistant constitute the office personnel. The assistant swings open the half door that separates his office from the *alcalde's* and says that the *alcalde* is free. After shaking hands, the *alcalde* sits back at his desk, and the person sits in an adjacent chair. The office entrance is a step away.

The Shape of San Pedro

As a place, San Pedro locates and houses its town activities in conformity with a strong Spanish-American cultural tradition and within the narrow, economic confines of a developing country. These two factors of cultural tradition and relative poverty give a distinctive, Colombian cast to San Pedro's universal status of being a town. The resultant vector of tradition, poverty, and activity is the shape of San Pedro.

The dominant quality of the shape is the perfect rectangularity of intersecting streets. At the fringes of the town, hills, creek, and highway disturb the rectangularity, but at the center the pattern reaches perfection with the foursquare plaza. The plaza's rectangularity is curiously emphasized by the circular park, centered in the plaza like a huge, green dot.

Bounded on all sides by buildings and punctuated with the park, the plaza is an architectural expression of social proximity and intimacy. It is the material set on which many *sanpedranos* act out a portion of their daily lives. On weekdays townsmen crisscross its space, stumbling slightly on the rock strewed dirt streets as they search for the *alcalde*, tax collector, priest, or friend. In the evening, small children, in noisy, sexless packs, dash through the park and in between separate groups of teenage boys and girls who occasionally stop their strolling for a quick exchange of words. Women, for the first time in the day, throw open their houses and emerge to chat with the neighbors, while their more free ranging husbands move from park bench to bar for a beer and a game of billiards. Saturdays, activity in the plaza begins to increase after the midday stoppage of work, and an infrequent movie of Mexican cowboys shown at the parish hall may prolong the night until the late hour of ten. Sundays, the culmination of the week, start with the priest's voice booming out commands to come to mass from the loud-speaker in the church tower. Hill farmers, having ridden their horses down from the isolated settlements for the weekend's shopping and recreation, cross the plaza; their machetes, encased in decorative holsters, swing briskly at their sides. Carefully attired with white and black mantillas over their heads, women patiently wait in church for mass to begin. As soon as the bell announces the beginning of the rite, the less pious men crowd into the church and stand begrudingly at the back. After mass and a brief chat at the church doorsteps, the men scatter into the bars for a hard afternoon's drinking of *aguardiente* (a clear, sneakingly potent rum). The women, temporarily freed of household chores, linger about for longer conversations. At twilight the *municipio* band comes to the park to play a concert of martial music and occasionally include in their repertoire the official hymn of San Pedro. Composed by the band director and the high school principal, the song moves to a rousing finale:

> Hail! Hail! Immortal land of my birth.
> Today your sons with pride proclaim,
> In words of love will always exclaim,
> That you are a symbol of Eden on earth.

The geographic form and function of San Pedro. (Photograph by Thomas Schorr.)

By late Sunday evening the men begin to wander home, the jukeboxes less frequently blare out a Mexican *corrido* or a Colombian *cumbia*, and finally the bar owners slam and lock their doors.

The different activities of San Pedro, being those of a small, poor town, do not have sufficient strength to demand special housing. A similar architectural style encases distinct activities and gives the town a deceptively uniform appearance. The main exception is the church. In Colombia, religious, Catholic, activity must be housed in a form that indicates its unique quality. The San Pedro church makes a brave attempt to fulfill that imperative. It presents to the plaza a neat facade of imitation brick carefully painted on sturdy adobe, wattle and daub walls. On the top of its bell tower is a neon cross. Its gaudy blue glow is marred by the unconcerned flickering of one arm. Adjacent to the church is the residence of the parish priest. Outside of a store-house of a merchant-farmer, the parish residence is the only two story building in town. The parish hall joins the residence, and the priest uses it to show an occasional movie and to dispense food and anti-Communist "comic" books, both originating in the United States. The local community action committee, the *junta comunal*, infrequently rents the hall for fund raising ventures, but the priest prefers to use it for affairs that will contribute to the church's treasury.

All other nonfamilial activities occur in buildings that bear a strong resemblance to the family house—a rectangular adobe brick structure with a double pitched, tile roof and tile floors. Only a vaguely fortlike facade distinguishes the present *alcaldía* from an adjacent family house. Perhaps indicating a surge in the secular arm of Colombian society, a new *alcaldía* with its own "office" architecture is being built. However, progress is slow and irregular because, say the *sanpedranos*, the politicians of Cali tend to their own nests first. Other buildings, whose style is even more domestic, house additional *municipio* and *departamento* offices. Squeezed into corner rooms of these buildings are the communication links: the telegraph office, the post office, and San Pedro's single telephone. The telephone is commanded by a young lady. When she receives a call for a townsman, she grabs the first person passing by and tells him, "They are calling Don Ramiro." The person finds Don Ramiro and passes on the information.

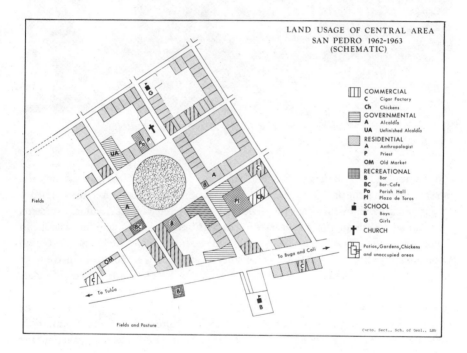

San Pedro has two elementary schools for its boys and girls. As if to give further rigor to the separation of the sexes, the buildings are located at either end of the town. Both structures are well kept, and their outside walls bear cheerful coats of pink and blue pastels. The coats of arms of various Colombian cities are painted in vivid colors on walls of the boys' school and give it a certain freshness. The boys' school is the larger and was recently constructed with money donated by a local *hacendado*. To testify to the benefactor's generosity the building bears his name and his statue shares the playground with one of the Holy Mother.

The two public schools offer the basic five-year program in the principal skills of reading, writing, and mathematics and in the primary subjects of history,

Waiting to see the doctor at the health center.

geography, and Catholicism. Students in the surrounding rural areas of the *municipio* finish the first two years in their community schools and then transfer to San Pedro. Following the completion of the elementary curriculum, students are eligible to attend the six years of secondary education offered in schools in Tuluá and Buga. The supervisor of the San Pedro school system, Señor Guido Ospina—who also writes about local history—estimates that 30 to 40 percent of the *municipio* population are illiterate. Don Guido tries to combat both illiteracy and the lackadaisical preschool environment with knowledge gained from the special courses that he attended at Bogotá. He is not satisfied with his success; he charges that the *sanpedrano* does not have sufficient culture to appreciate education. Like the principal of Mainstreet Elementary, Don Guido labors away at the darkness.

The recreational centers, the bars and the cafe, and the commercial concerns, the cigar factories, the barbershops, the stores, reside in family-style housing. The owners, especially of the commercial enterprises, live in adjacent rooms, and their wives and children constitute the nucleus of the work force. The building that once housed the stalls of the weekly market is now the home of several families. The specialized nature of raising chickens on a commercial scale has intruded into the uniformity of the San Pedro scene and the long, narrow chicken houses that appear within the town blocks and on the outskirts softly contrast with the prevalent domestic style.

Medical treatment is another specialty that San Pedro adds to its list of town activities. Appropriate to its poor town status, San Pedro has a young intern who commutes from Buga. He divides his time between the social security clinic and the health station. The clinic serves salaried workers, such as the cigar workers, who participate in the national health program; the health station attends to the remainder of the population. Both facilities are in buildings which are distinguishable from adjacent homes only by their respective signs. San Pedro does not have a hospital. For that type of care and for private doctors the *sanpedrano* travels to Buga.

A woman, born in Bogotá, who is variously called a *curandera* (curer), a *yerbatera* or *botánica* (herbalist), and an *enfermera* (nurse) is much below the doctor in the number of patients she treats. She refers to herself in more simple terms, as a seller of drugs, and she prescribes for the minor illnesses that the townfolk and the rural people bring to her. She also has a store of knowledge about medicinal plants and will dispense these if she has them on hand.

Mothers have their own repertoire of cures that include both pills and plants. Once they have exhausted their treatment of, for example, diarrhea, they may take their baby to the drug seller, but more commonly they go to the young intern—or if they can afford it, to the doctors in Buga. Corresponding to these different types of curing resources, medical knowledge possessed by the townspeople seems to be a relatively unsystematized mixture of industrial-modern and agrarian-traditional. Headaches can be cured either with aspirin or by cabbage leaves. Infectious germs arise out of the newly wet soil or from mosquitos. Yellow fever produces malaria, and mosquitos bring both malaria and anemia. As it does to the people of Mainstreet, the common cold tests the *sanpedranos'* ingenuity. One of the many remedies is to drink a tea made of the bitter orange boiled in sugared water followed with an aspirin. The aspirin is a necessary ingredient as it makes the person sweat out the fever associated with the cold.

The final special activity that occupies space in San Pedro is the burial of the dead. The holy ground of the consecrated cemetery is the first sign of San Pedro that a traveler from Buga sees. An imitation brick wall encases the grounds, and over the large, imposing gate the Virgin and her Child stand guard. Inside, the high vaults preserve the sanctified dead. Across town and in the unconsecrated ground next to the now decaying slaughter house lie two other *sanpedranos*. Their aberrant lives as bandits prohibited their burial with ordinary townsmen. Now and again, at the foot of the small gravestones flowers appear, brought by relatives who remember the bandits as sons or husbands.

The square cornered shape of San Pedro, maximally expressed in the layout of the town, is duplicated in the grouping of rectangular houses around the sides of a block and is duplicated once more in the arrangement of rooms around the patio of a house. The minimal architectural unit of San Pedro is the house, and its inhabitants form the town's most compact social entity.

To enter the house the family members go directly from the street into a parlorlike room. Crossing this room they emerge into the sheltered sunlight of the patio. Along the sides, either a wing of the house or a solid fence blocks away the street and the neighbors. At the back the larger houses frequently have another rectangular set of rooms, but even the smallest houses attempt to complete the enclosure with a fence. Beyond the back rooms or fence is an area where privacy

The unconsecrated graves of Sanpedrano *bandits.*

is not so highly valued. This is the *solar,* a patch of ground that contains the garden, the fruit trees, and the few hens that every family has.

To the street the San Pedro house presents a solid wall of brick, adobe, or wattle and daub, glaring with a white painted face trimmed in blue or pink pastels. Its openings restricted to tiny windows and closed doors, the house stands uncompromisingly against the curious glance, the casual word, the social chaos of the street. To the family, it offers the informal intimacy of the patio. Potted plants, carefully attended by its mistress, relax the patio's angularity, and in one of the sheltered nooks the family sits to eat. The house is primarily, and especially for men, a place to eat and to sleep. In the larger structures, the front room serves as a true visiting parlor, but even these frequently have a bed in the corner. Men do all their drinking and most of their chatting out of the home. Women prefer to move chairs out on the sidewalk for an evening's exchange with their female friends. During the day the house is shut. At night, fearing the thieves that it may bring, the inhabitants crowd themselves into their small bedrooms. They carefully bolt even the patio doors and close the smallest window in order to make secure their withdrawal from the world.

Los Sanpedranos

As a place, the shape of San Pedro is a crystallization of cultural tradition, relative poverty, and town status. As a people, the *sanpedranos* speak, think, and act in forms also casted by tradition, poverty, and status. Yet the inhabitants are more heterogeneous than the place where they live. The quiet wars of individuals, their private tragedies and triumphs, react on the forms and corrode the pure models into the complex shapes of distinctive people.

There is Don Hernán, the *alcalde*. A mixture of informality and restraint, he moves easily through the town. He stops to give a kid a few centavos for a coke; he goes into *El Bar Central* for a beer but never gets visibly drunk. He is *una persona muy formal*, "a very formal person," friendly, kind, but correct. In his own words, he is the father of San Pedro; he speaks to the governor of the Valle about the needs of his town and *municipio*. An owner of a sizeable area of land in the *municipio*, he lives immediately outside of town. Yet he and his wife feel middle class, and they talk about moving into Buga, his birthplace. He launched a vigorous campaign to purchase a small, waist-high refrigerator, one of the few in town, that the anthropologist had bought in a used appliance store in Tuluá. Don Hernán, by overpowering the owner with free drinks and demanding pleas that friends sell cheaper to each other, defeated his competitor, the *municipio* judge. Before the sale was finalized his wife took her friends to the owner's house to hear their admiring comments about her useful adornment.

There is Pedro, who worked for a while in a cigar factory in a position that was a strange combination of flunky and foreman. Before he left to work in a leather shop in Tuluá, Pedro liked to talk about philosophy and culture, about Henry Wallace's trip to Colombia and about the singing of Nelson Eddy. Pedro's drinking buddy, who does not care for abstract discussions, is Ramón, the furniture maker. Ramón keeps magazine pictures of furniture styles under his bed and pulls them out to show to his prospective customers. Despite the choice that he offers, he does not seem to be able to escape from producing a monumental style he calls Louis XV. An unexpected customer or two allowed him to expand into the bar business, but Pedro, Ramón, and other friends drank up both profit and credit, so he, his wife, and child left town one quiet night.

Don Carlos, the tailor, came from Cali, searching, as did Ramón, for a place without competition. Don Carlos, however, is like the *alcalde*; he is a formal person, entitled to respect. When he talks about Spanish, the language of love, or about English, the language of Shakespeare, people listen—even and especially teenage boys. Don Carlos' father has a good position in an insurance company in Tuluá and has traveled in the United States. But for some reason Carlos does not care for office work and wearing suits every day. At times he even becomes bored with tailoring and dreams of expanding his two or three goats and his small flock of ducks. Don Carlos protects his only child from seeing the pictures of decapitated bandits in the newspapers and does not like for her to read comics. He has little fear that she will be a victim of some woman's evil eye, but he prefers not to have many people around her.

Chucho is a prosperous native son of San Pedro. He owns one of the largest cigar factories in San Pedro and has recently expanded into raising chickens. During the day he strolls about in a half-opened sport shirt. At night he sits in the park quietly explaining to his Catholic friends the profundities of their faith, how the faith prohibits them from killing and how it instructs them to help their neighbors. He rarely drinks and never goes to church. Prosperous, correct, and formal, Chucho is only occasionally called Don. Perhaps it is because Chucho is

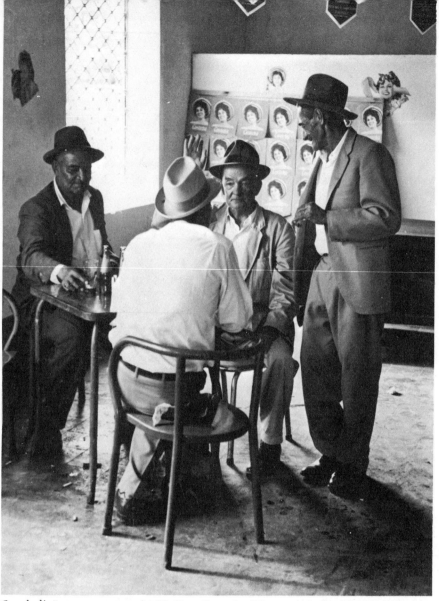

Concluding an argument in El Bar Central. (Photograph by Thomas Schorr.)

a nickname for Jesús and "Don Chucho" sounds a little silly, or perhaps it is due to his youth and his life as a hometown boy.

Each of Chucho's siblings were born in a different *departamento*. One older sister was born in Tolima and moved with the family to Valle and to San Pedro. She married an *alcalde* of San Pedro, but before their children were grown, he died. Her oldest son, Seneca, became her supporter and her guardian. Perhaps because he was the son of a former *alcalde* and a godson of a large *hacendado*, Seneca secured a minor position in the *municipio* bureaucracy. He has the curious job of inspector of the forest, curious because only in the bandit-infested mountains is there any forest. As the young, unmarried son of a poor widow, Seneca was a person in which one could have *confianza* but not *respeto*. People joked with him and called him by his nickname, Carate, because of the spots on his legs left by a skin disease. Then Seneca won approximately $1000 in a lottery. He married, remodeled his mother's house, and lowered his what-is-in-it-for-me antennae. Now some people are calling him Don.

Señora Leonor Beserra came from Palmira with her common-law husband. He decided he did not love her anymore and so found another woman in San Pedro. As a tough, durable grandmother, the Señora heads, but does not dictate, her remaining children. Her older sons have left San Pedro; her eldest daughter has made a good marriage to Chucho, but the next daughter was not so lucky and brought her son back to the Señora's house. Her pride is Ninivé, a vivacious, nineteen year old señorita who considers everything "divine." Ninivé has a good secretarial position in Palmira but returns each weekend to her mother's house. Being a good daughter she pays her mother for room and meals. The Señora does not bother with the subtleties of thought. Upon hearing that Holy Week in the United States is not like the elaborate, death-oriented, Colombian parade of images, she concludes that people lied when they said that President Kennedy was a Catholic.

A next door neighbor of the Señora is Ramiro, whom she calls Don and who addresses her as Doña or Misia. He chats with Don Carlos about the lack of interest that Colombians have in their own culture and how they throw away their own music in order to listen to the voices of movie stars. Ramiro, however, is more caustic; his bitterness runs deeper. His repeated demands for *una fuerza brutal*, a brutal force to end the anarchic state of contemporary Colombia are too spiteful, too full of acid, to attract listeners. Ramiro prides himself on his *antioqueño* ancestry. As an object lesson he points to a native *sanpedrano*, a Tascón, who does not work the land that his well-to-do father left him but runs a small store. "What is a man with property doing selling candy to children?" Ramiro contemptuously asked.

Following his unsuccessful attempt to study medicine at the University of Cauca in Popayán and his equally temporary effort at marriage, Ramiro has passed in and out of San Pedro, staying for a while with his retired father, then moving on, looking for a better position, a new opportunity. He worked in a Cali hotel as a desk clerk, failed in an attempt to attach himself to a visiting American university professor, then returned to San Pedro. He worked with the anthropologist for about two weeks, but the pay was too low, so he devoted all of his time to buying and selling livestock. One day, reporting that the new minister of agriculture, an old school friend, had called him, he left for Bogotá.

Don Guido, the school director, is an Ospina. The Ospinas, according to Don Guido, came from Spain to Colombia some 200 years ago. They have never mixed with Indians and prefer to marry members of another pure family, the Tascons. Don Guido, however, found an *antioqueña* more to his liking. Commenting not so much about his own children but about children in general, he says that they no longer believe in witches or *duendes* (malicious, elflike creatures). In fact they do not even believe in the police. The children of today do not respect authority, either public or parental, as they did in his youth. The flaunting of

San Pedro band celebrating the election of the Queen of Poultry. (Photograph by Thomas Schorr.)

authority is the result of modern times, a product of the *cocacolisación* process, a modernity characterized by soft drink and easy virtue.

There are others in San Pedro, like the farmer from Boyacá, who plants his maize with an iron-tipped digging stick when the moon is waning; or like the agriculturalist from Roldanillo, who brought his special training in raising poultry to San Pedro and developed his own breed of chickens, but who lives in a tacky house of wattle and daub while his chickens eat in the neat splendor of solid brick. Still others appear for the moment and then are gone, like the friendly night watchman from Tuluá, who looked out at San Pedro one night at 9:30 from his station at the social security clinic and remarked, "This town is truely sleeping." Or like the man from another city, Cartago, who comes each weekend to drink in small-town comfort. Or like the man who continued to sit with the anthropologist at a bar table when everyone else was out in the street praying to God to stop the earthquake. In stunned bravery produced by *aguardiente*, they turned to each other; one, with a lift of his glass, saying, *"Salud"*; the other replying, "Bottoms up."

Made restless by the strains and gaps in the Colombian socioeconomic structure, people move in and out of San Pedro. They come into town not in response to its economic pulling power, for even the largest cigar factory employs only about thirty people, but rather they come because they have failed elsewhere, failed in the sense of unsuccessful competition for very scarce jobs or in the more diffused sense of satisfaction with their former positions. They try to find a nook in San Pedro, a piece of unused land back behind town or a portion of the town's small income to support their store or their trade. As did Don Carlos, some approximate their destiny; others, like Pedro, Ramón, and Ramiro, seem damned to wander through the interstices of Colombian society.

Officials also join in the flow of persons in and out of San Pedro. Those who hold appointive positions, such as the priest, the *municipio* judge, and the *alcalde,* are particularly mobile. These people move from town to town like checkers on a giant board. In 1962–1963, one priest, a taciturn man who restricted his role to the confines of the altar and confession booth, was replaced with a more exuberant man, whose voice, on especially bright mornings at 6:00, boomed out of the loud-speaker: "People of San Pedro. Awake! Children to school. Men to their jobs!" The relaxed, salty *municipio* judge left for another town and a mildly snobbish person from Palmira took his place. Don Hernán had been the *alcalde* for a year; one of his predecessors, Seneca's father, had either been an *alcalde* or a judge in some 14 Valle *municipios.*

The swirl of people around San Pedro is not recent. Of its 213 heads of families 53 percent were born out of the town and the *municipio.* Another 36 percent were born in *departamentos* other than Valle, and nearly all of these were from the *antioqueño* region of Antioquia and Caldas.

Throughout these movements San Pedro has gained more than it has lost. In 1938 the town, exclusive of the rural *municipio* area, had 677 people. Twenty six years later, in 1964, the town contained 1527, a respectable increase of 56 percent. This increase, however respectable, pales in comparison with the 86 percent addition in Cali's population, an addition which changed Cali from a provincial city of 88,366 in 1938 to a full-grown, urban complex of 618,215 in 1964.

By looking at a *sanpedrano* one cannot distinguish him either in physical type or in dress from a Cali urbanite. Only the predominance of the machete indicates that many *sanpedranos* are farmers or farm laborers. Skin color ranges from a perfect white to a deep, glowing brown; facial features and hair form are generally Caucasian, and there is even a blond or two. The *sanpedrano* population is probably a tri-ethnic mixture. Through some strange quirk of genetics the combination produces women whose striking appearances overpower that of the men. The *sanpedranos* lump their genetic heterogeneity into a single category, white. They never refer to themselves as mestizo or mulattoes, and a person classed as white but who has a very dark skin is simply called a brown, *moreno.* Contemptuous of Negroes, who are lazy, the *sanpedranos* are equally scornful of Indians, who are savages. None would dream, however, of having a separate school for Negroes, and an Indian, as long as he is not the bow-and-arrow kind, would be welcomed in any bar.

The daily costume for men in San Pedro is a light sport shirt and dark slacks. Young men wear the shirt with the top button loose so as to display the religious medal around their neck. They like their slacks baggy and pegged at the ankle. For manual labor in the streets or in the fields, they take off their shoes and put on a many-patched variant of daily wear. For occasions demanding special dress, the men wear suits with or without a tie; young men like to add a bit of flare by draping the coat over their shoulders. Men of status often put on an appropriately ponderous felt hat with a flat brim for trips out of town.

The everyday garment for women is a cotton dress, sleeveless with a tight bodice. Special occasions for young women demand a silk dress that emphasizes a prominent bosom and equaly bulging buttocks. Older women, when they go to Tuluá or Buga, dress more sedately in loose flowing black. In 1962–1963 the up-to-date bouffant hair style and shift decorated the teenage girls. However, one could still get a glimpse of an old woman who, with a plain dress draped over her angular frame and with a cigar clenched in her teeth, gave the unshakable appearance that she and her kind would live forever.

Mothers wrap their babies and often swaddle them, but once the baby starts to crawl, it is conveniently left naked from the waist down until it is toilet trained. Young children are allowed to go barefoot, but the family makes a great effort to dress everyone, even the smallest infant, in socks and shoes for mass, fiestas, and trips to cities.

The economic ladder in San Pedro begins with a shoeless family and extends up to the lower-middle-class rung on the national scale. Representative of this lower-middle-class position is the Tascón that Ramiro dismissed as a seller of candy. His land holdings, although not on the scale of the *hacendados* in the valley plain, are sizeable. He drives to the city in his truck, and he owns a well-kept house with a parlour decorated with modern, plastic-covered chairs and coffee table. Important people, such as the director of a Tuluá high school, gather there. At the economic bottom of San Pedro is the home of an old woman, who, at the age of ninety, still moves about. In fact, she is reputed to have ridden a broomstick to the top of a neighbor's house. However, her reputation as a witch has gained her little, for her house is a sad affair of split bamboo walls and dirt floors. A single tap in the small, cluttered yard provides her family with water. There is nothing neat, quaint, or industrious about her dwelling; it is simply a dirty shack.

Sanpedranos describe their town as a place of tranquility, a pleasant spot whose inhabitants are in the state of moral health. Because of these virtues, *violencia* has never erupted on its streets. As townsmen, the *sanpedranos* are different from the "simple people," the "everyday, ordinary folk," the *campesinos* or peasants, who live outside of town. The *sanpedrano*, even though he may farm for a living, lives in town. He is an urbanite.

Once he has explained how pleasant San Pedro is, the townsman proceeds to hurl caustic comments at his town and at his neighbors. "San Pedro," he sarcastically remarks, "is a backward, unprogressive place. If you come back in five years, it will still be the same." Another townsman, devoid of pity, adds, "People, here, are poor. They don't know how to behave; they don't have culture." Still another warns, "Do not allow just anyone in town to look inside your house.

They will see where things are and return at night to steal them." Bitter comment piles upon bitter comment. "Yesterday you could honor a person's word; today you can't." "Don't place your trust in just any *sanpedrano*; he will exploit you and steal your belongings." "The Church teaches us to feed and clothe the stranger who comes to our door, but today this is not possible; the 'needy' stranger is probably a thief." "When someone knocks at your door at night, don't open it. The person is surely a bandit, who has come to rob and to kill."

These black commentaries on life fit the behavioral patterns of the towns-people far closer than the platitudes of tranquility and moral health. Men drink hard and aggressively. Women guard their babies against the evil eye of a passing acquaintance. Arguments are won through verbally dominating the antagonist; word is stacked upon word even in ordinary conversation, and we are reminded of the people of Aritama, of *violencia*, of the *bogotazo*, and even of Mainstreet, riots, and assassinations.

In the manner that Mainstreet is American, San Pedro, both as a place and as a people, is Colombian. It is not typically Colombian, but the activities that *sanpedranos* do and the ways in which they meditate on those actions are part and parcel of Colombia's cultural tradition and its contemporary structure. Tradition and structure dictate the economic, political, religious, and familial roles that *sanpedranos* play. The depiction of these roles is the task of the next four chapters.

3

The Economic Side

V IEWED ECONOMICALLY, the town of San Pedro is the place of residence
of individuals engaged in different activities. *Sanpedranos* farm, as owners,
sharecroppers, or laborers; they make cigars, as factory owners or employees; and, if they are abandoned or widowed women, run their house on money
scraped up from this or that source. Some work in the *municipio* or *departamento*
offices; some run stores, sell livestock, repair engines, drive trucks, or build houses.
Others cut hair, repair shoes, or make clothes. They are participants in a capitalistic
system that is undergoing an elite-controlled modernization, and they try to hedge
against the built-in insecurity through exploration of the nooks and crannies of the
local setting. They raise a variety of crops, expand from producing cigars to raising
chickens, borrow money from the *Caja Agraria* (Agrarian Bank), sharecrop with a
landowner, and, when all else fails, play the lottery. Since they are members of a
nation-wide economic system, their exploitation of local opportunities relates them
to individuals and organizations located in other towns and cities. A farmer sells his
surplus maize to a private buyer in Tuluá, a chicken producer sends his birds to
Bogotá, and a store owner buys his supplies from a Buga wholesale dealer.

The *sanpedranos* are also Colombians and their private welfare rises and
falls according to the performance of the nation's economy. In certain ways the
town has prospered. Each home has at least one water faucet, the cigar factories
have expanded, and the chicken industry is flourishing. Yet the *sanpedranos* are not
impressed. As they ponder upon their economic state, as they catalog and evaluate
their activities, they are critical of the efforts of their fellow townsmen and
devastating in their attacks upon their nation.

Farms, Chickens, and Horse Traders

Like Don Carlos, the tailor, with his two or three goats and his small flock
of ducks, most *sanpedranos* attempt to supplement the family income with a few

Spreading tobacco for drying.

animals and a garden in the back yard. Nearly all have three or four chickens which produce an occasional egg before they land in the pot. A particularly lucky family may have a hog which they will stake out in a ditch so that it can enjoy a refreshing wallow. Several families raise a vegetable and fruit garden in their *solar*. Under the directorship of the house wife, these gardens receive varying degrees of attention, and the best ones decrease the family's grocery expenses, but none are large enough or receive sufficient care to make the family independent of the stores.

Agriculture as an occupation, rather than as a lackadaisical supplement to another primary income, is the work of 25 percent of the 213 family heads in San Pedro. Of this group, nineteen own land, eleven sharecrop, and twenty-five are laborers. The land that these town agriculturists cultivate is for the most part located directly outside San Pedro. Bordering the town side of the valley highway, the farms cover the small amount of flat land alongside the now dry, now flooding San Pedro creek and extend up into the foothills of the Cordillera Central. Few town-farmers work the flat land of the Cauca valley floor, and the valley highway decisively marks the boundary between the land of the town-farmer and the large acreage of the valley *hacendado* or the small plots of the *campesino*. Although there is little in technique or in acreage that separates the town-farmer from the *campesino*, the townsmen—at least to the townsmen—are urbanites, and the *campesinos*, rustic peasants.

Frequently a farmer will work a plot near town and have another back in the foothills, but the total size does not usually exceed 10 *plazas* (1 *plaza* is 1.6 acres). In a class by himself, one *sanpedrano* owns the surprising total of 600 *plazas*. Four hundred of these *plazas*, located near the mountain city of Sevilla, he has had to abandon because of *violencia*. He has an additional 100 *plazas* in the coastal *municipio* of Buenaventura and a 100 *plazas* around San Pedro.

If a *sanpedrano* farmer has not inherited land or if the plot that he has is too small to support his family, he has three alternatives for securing additional acreage: he may purchase it, rent it, or work it on the shares. To purchase land means to search for very scarce capital. The national government has created the *Caja Agraria* to make more capital available through loans at low interest. At least one *sanpedrano* is using money from the *Caja* to buy a few more *plazas*, and five families are buying their houses with *Caja* loans. A few farmers have enough money to rent land, but the most viable alternative, since it requires even less cash than renting, is to sharecrop. The farmer and the landowner agree that the farmer will work the land by the thirds, which means the cultivator pays all the expenses and gets two thirds of the crop, or by the halves, where the owner contributes to the expenses and so gets half the crop.

To assist him in his work, the farmer calls upon the "free" labor of his unmarried sons. If his sons are too small or have left home, he may hire a laborer by the job, day, or week. The laborer is nearly always a non-relative. Some argue that if he were a relative the kinship tie would safeguard the employer from exploitation, but kinship, beyond that of the nuclear family, is a fragile thing in San Pedro. Even those who advise hiring relatives, hire non-kinsmen.

The town-farmer, owner or sharecropper, plants a variety of crops. Somewhere on his land he will usually have a combination of tobacco, tomatoes, beans, coffee, plaintains, bananas, and sugar cane. All farmers plant maize and an account of how Simeón Gutiérrez, Anibal Pinzón, and the Lozano brothers work this crop will portray in detail the practice of *sanpedrano* agriculture.

Simeón Gutiérrez is an unusual farmer for San Pedro. Instead of learning agricultural practices from his father, he received formal training from a school in Roldanillo, where he was born. He calls himself a veterinarian and has developed his own breed of chickens. He obtains the high yield hybrid seed from the agricultural experiment station in Palmira, and when he is ready to plant his two *plazas* located just behind the cemetery, he pays no attention to the moon. To prepare the plot and to plant it, he rents the *alcalde*'s tractor. The tractor comes equipped with a driver, who is a person with a unique and valuable skill in San Pedro, almost as scarce as tractors. He instructs the driver to make the rows a meter apart so that the maize will receive sufficient sunlight to develop into strong plants.

Because of San Pedro's geographical position, Señor Gutiérrez and the other farmers have two maize seasons, the *traviesa*, which is from March to August, and the *cosecha*, from September to February. When the maize has matured, Gutiérrez hires a helper as his sons are too young to work. With the helper's assistance, he shells the grain with a hand-driven mechanical sheller. The maize harvest goes to feed his chickens, his main source of income, and his family.

Certain *sanpedrano* dishes require the removal of the hard kernel surrounding the soft, fruit part of the grain, and for this job Gutiérrez takes his maize to a store owner who has a gas driven machine (*trilladora*) in a back room of his store-house. Neither Señora Gutiérrez nor any other housewife in San Pedro are forced to grind corn by hand. Maize is a particularly healthy food, according to Gutiérrez, because it contains an abundance of vitamin A, and he agrees with Señor Pinzón and others that the hairs on the ear are good for kidney ailments.

Señor Anibal Pinzón is from Boyacá and given the Indian cast to his face one would expect him to be taciturn and passive. Instead he is a lively man, much more so than Gutiérrez, and talks continually. He is a friend of Seneca, and they traveled to Bogotá to take Seneca's youngest sister to the convent that Pinzón's daughter is in.

In addition to the *plaza* near his house, Pinzón has rented another *plaza*. He has rented it only for one harvest in order to check its fertility. It probably is a fertile spot because it once was a house site, but the houses were destroyed to clear a passage for high voltage cables.

Señor Pinzón plants the seeds saved from a previous crop. Because of their differential demands for sunlight, he plants yellow maize in the center of the field and white maize along the edges. If the ground is dry, he first soaks the seed in kerosene to protect them against insects. If the ground is wet, he may take the trouble of sprouting his seeds in water before planting them. When planting sprouted seed, care is needed not to break off the tiny stem or else the seed will produce only roots. After the hot, back-breaking job of preparing his field with a large bladed hoe (*azadón*), Pinzón plants his maize with an iron-tipped digging stick. He staggers his seeds so that the heat of the day can enter from as many angles as possible. If the seeds are planted in a perfect rectangle, then the heat can enter only through two sides. To produce properly, maize must be planted when the moon is old and waning. If the moon is new and waxing, all the energy will go into the stalk and the ears will be tiny with widely dispersed kernels. Pinzón plants beans and manioc between the maize stalks, but he has to wait until the maize is tall because the maize tassel is fierce and will damage the more placid beans. He weeds the field with his machete.

All these things about maize Pinzón's father taught him in Boyacá. He passes on the information to his smaller sons who help him when they are not in school. The older sons have left home, one is working land that he has rented, one has joined the police force, and the other has entered the army. The maize that Pinzón produces goes to feed his family. To shell the maize, he puts the ears in a burlap sack and beats the sack with a stick.

The Lozano brothers run a bigger operation than either Gutiérrez or Pinzón. Their father owns some 30 *plazas* near town and smaller acreage across the highway on the valley plain. The larger holding is devoted primarily to pastures for fifteen dairy cows. The eldest brother owns a battered, but serviceable Chevrolet truck. He wants to trade it for a tractor, but until then they rent the *alcalde*'s machine and its driver.

The Lozanos are exceptional in that the three brothers work together and live together on their father's land and in his house. The father, although still vigorous, has all but retired. He has taught his sons all that he knows about agricultural practices and has delegated to his eldest son the responsibility for running the farm and the dairy. This son seems to have peaceful relations with the next two brothers, who are in their early twenties and who assist him. The total family consists of a grandmother, the two parents, the three brothers, the wife of the eldest brother and her child, and a much younger brother. Perhaps it is the size of their holdings, their dairy, and their relative prosperity that accounts for their familial unity.

The Lozano brothers are closer to Pinzón than Gutiérrez in the selection of seed maize and in their belief concerning the influence of the moon. Although they know of hybrid seed, they prefer to obtain a variety they call While Limanian from a man who has a reputation for good seeds. They resemble Gutiérrez in cultivation techniques. The tractor that they rent prepares the seed bed, plants, and cultivates the 7 *plazas* presently in maize. The brothers hire workers to give the maize an additional cleaning with machetes and also to harvest it. For shelling they pay a man from Tuluá to come to San Pedro with his motor driven mechanical sheller.

The maize harvest is sufficiently great to produce a surplus beyond the needs of their home and of their dairy. They sell this surplus to the person who pays them the best price. They do not give special preference to relatives, but like all other *sanpedranos* they operate on the capitalist principle of selling to highest bidder. Usually the highest bidder is another private capitalist, a merchant in Tuluá; occasionally when the price falls, it is the governmental National Institute of Supplies.

Señor Gutiérrez is a quiet, almost sullen man. On a rare occasion he strolls through the *plaza* in the evening, but he hardly ever goes into the bars, even on Sunday. His house, a converted chicken barn left over from less prosperous days, sits along on a slight rise on the fringe of town. Between his house and the town is his justification for being Simeón Gutiérrez, his chicken house. In this tightly constructed brick building, he devotes his time to the careful tending of his own breed of chickens, the Sime. Other persons in the town watch him closely, and the success of his efforts have stimulated some of them to try this new way of making money.

Chucho talked the question of chickens over with Climaco, his partner in the cigar business, and they decided to go ahead. Chucho hired a carpenter to construct a house of sturdy bamboo, wire, and wattle and daub on an unoccupied spot in his backyard. He and Climaco, who scraped up enough pesos from the earnings of his own small cigar factory and from his most recent tomato crop, bought some 800 chicks from Simeón. Simeón instructed them to provide the chicks with constant water and feed and to have electric lights burning at night so the birds would eat continually. Once the chickens were large and fat, the partners sold them to a man who was filling a truck bound for Bogotá. The endeavor was so successful that the partners immediately bought another batch from Simeón. Other people were experiencing the same success, and presently poultry—either for meat or eggs—has almost replaced cigar making as the principal industry in the town. Twelve heads of families have commercial chicken raising, either as a primary or as a secondary source of income.

Ten male heads of *sanpedrano* families buy and sell crops and livestock. The livestock traders buy horses, hogs, donkeys, and a few cattle, fatten the animals, and then sell them. The profit of such ventures is found mainly in the art of playing the market, of buying cheap and selling dear. The Tuluá livestock market, held every last Tuesday in the month, is the scene of such bargaining. The traders mingle with the large rancher, who brings in zebu beef cattle by the truck load, and with the small farmer, who has a colt or a pig to sell. As they mingle, the *sanpedranos* try to pick up a good buy or to conclude a sharp sell.

The traders may act as spokesman for a third party, as did Marco Aurelio, the man Don Julio authorized to sell the anthropologist's horse. Don Julio inherited the job of looking after the horse when Ramiro, his son, left for Bogotá. Marco Aurelio told Don Julio that he had found a man who would offer 600 pesos (roughly $60). Although the anthropologist wanted 700, the price that he had paid, Don Julio advised him to sell. He cautioned, "*Vale más un pajaro en la mano que cien volando.*"* So Marco sold the horse for 600 and received a 10 percent commission. All were satisfied except the anthropologist who, on the realization that he had lost 160 pesos on the deal, could only mumble to himself, "Well, that's the way the cookie crumbles."

Cigars and Billiard Cues

Tobacco and cigars have had a long history in San Pedro and in Colombia. Before the coffee revolution of the nineteenth century, tobacco was Colombia's main product. In San Pedro, although threatened by the more recent chicken industry, the manufacturing of cigars is still the town's largest industry. As if in attempt to solidify the status of tobacco, the *municipio* council awarded it a place on the town shield. The shield is quartered into four fields and depicted on the fields are an agricultural scene, a cannon—commemorating a nearby battle in the late nineteenth century between the Liberals and the Conservatives—an ear of corn, and a tobacco plant.

Two types of factories produce cigars. There are the three minute, part-time operators such as Climaco's. He sets up his production line of two or three people in a spare room of his house when he has accumulated sufficient leaves. Climaco's partner, Chucho, and Mario Tascón operate the two much larger, full-time factories, which together employ fifty-seven workers.

Chucho worked in Mario's factory until he had learned the process and then set up his own factory. On the street in front of his house, he nearly always has drying mats covered with chopped tobacco leaves, and inside along the sheltered sides of the patio, he has several production lines going simultaneously. Making a cigar is a rapid affair once men have chopped the leaves into bits with their machetes. One person molds the bits into the body of the cigar, and another compresses the body and covers it with a single leaf. This final stage calls for the skilled manipulation of small hand rollers, and consequently the operator receives more money. Chucho pays his workers, not by the hour, but by the number of cigars they make in a day. Before he can ship the cigars to be sold in Cali, he

---

* Better one bird in the hand than one hundred flying.

Sanpedranas *making cigars.*

also has to pay a governmental tax graded according to the quality of the cigar. His best cigar, The Queen, sells for 15 centavos (almost 2 cents), and on these cigars he is taxed 35 pesos ($3.50) per thousand. Chucho would like to buy machines and reduce his production expenses, but he says he cannot because the Colombian government prohibits the importation of cigar machines.

Mario Tascón lives in Tuluá, where he has other business interests, and daily travels to his San Pedro cigar factory, which occupies a house located on the outskirts of town. He employs fewer people, twenty-two, than does Chucho but produces a better quality cigar from tobacco important from the Atlantic *departamento* of Barranquilla. His best cigar is a rum crook, La Cigalia, which sells for 25 centavos. Mario has a machine to render the leaves into bits, but the rest of the process is hand labor, which, according to Mario, makes a better cigar. In the familiar litany of the businessman, he bemoans the high governmental tax, because it keeps him from paying a higher salary to his workers. The low salary makes it difficult to get help.

The workers in the two large cigar factories are among the elite of the town laborers. They are participants in the national social security plan which guarantees them medical care, and their fairly steady income receives a yearly boost with a bonus at Christmas. Work in the factories is one of the few legitimate jobs that a San Pedro woman can hold outside of her house. Perhaps nearly half of the total work force in the two factories are women, and fourteen females heads of families, as contrasted to only nine male heads, find employment in the factories.

Señor José Rafael Rojas is the epitome of a small town captain of industry and the most representative of San Pedro's entrepreneurs. He is the owner of Indusrojas, an industry for producing billiard cues. Throughout Colombia men amuse themselves in bars playing billiards, and settlements much smaller than San Pedro have at least one table. Señor Rojas has effectively tied himself into this immense market. His factory occupies all of his patio of his house, and cue sticks overflow into the bedrooms. All steps in making the cues, except painting, are mechanized. Electric powered saws reduce the wood brought from Tuluá into long rectangular strips, and lathes turn the strips into cues.

Don José, in his own way, confronts the paradoxes that plague a developing country. In order to diversify its economy, Colombia needs to industrialize; it has to protect native industrialists from foreign competition. The things that it protects, the tips of cues and sandpaper, Don José needs. He can buy tips and paper made in Colombia, but according to him, they are not any good. These limitations are a constant irritation to him. "I understand," he says, "that Colombia has to produce its own goods, but what is being produced now is inferior. Of course in the future Colombia will manufacture first-class material, but now, here am I, trying to make a good cue with tips that break and sandpaper that tears."

A native of San Pedro, Señor Rojas is a bustling, talkative person, who prides himself as a self-made man. He employs two or three workers, but exclaims, "In this house everyone works! The smallest child can carry a stick, from here to there. Like the capitalists in the United States and in Japan, I built my factory up from nothing. I taught myself how to make cues, and it took me three days to make my first one. When I started, all the capital that I had was one peso and twenty centavos. Now my factory turns out many sticks in one day, and I am worth several thousand pesos."

The Market and the *Junta Comunal*

The image of a typical Colombian town always calls forth its market place. In small towns the weekly market is held in stalls temporarily set up in the plaza; in larger cities the daily market is in a large, barnlike structure subdivided into innumerable booths. The booths offer a wide range of vegetables, meat, fish, hardware, software, pots, and shirts. The market is an exciting place to be; the vision of so many different items crammed into one spot and the sanctioned duel of wills between the seller and the buyer serves to relieve, however briefly, the monotony of daily life. For a town, a bustling market is its reason for being, its justification for occupying space.

San Pedro is not typical; it is real. Because it is real, it is subject to the push and pull of contemporary developments. The developments have transformed San Pedro from a market center to a consumer suburb of Buga and particularly of Tuluá.

Not too long ago, prior to the 1950s, San Pedro had a weekly market. The structure that housed the merchants' stalls is still there, on the northern fringe of town, but now it is the residence of several families. The slaughter shed where cattle and hogs were butchered still occupies a spot in a grassy field east of town, but it is quickly falling apart. Once the main valley highway was paved and buses began to stop every fifteen minutes at San Pedro, the local market was doomed. For 5 cents a *sanpedrano* could ride the bus to Tuluá, fill her basket with a wide selection, see a bit of the city, and then for another nickel, return to San Pedro.

The two general stores in San Pedro, plus the four or five vegetable stalls in the front rooms of the sellers' houses, maintain a lingering market function. People from the isolated hill settlements come every Sunday to shop at these stores, but the expanding economic spheres of Tuluá and Buga are beginning to pull even these settlements into their orbits as new roads and buses make the cities accessible to the hill people.

The wilting of the market has left San Pedro without an outward sign of its economic self. The *Junta Comunal*, the Community Committee, is trying to restore the economic image of San Pedro and to reshape it into a concept of a community that helps itself. The idea that a community can use its own resources to improve itself does not come from a *sanpedrano* but from Colombia's elite. It is part of their modernizing package designed to combat local poverty and make communities less receptive to anti-elite sentiments and movements.

Julio César Tascón, the pleasant, soft-spoken owner of *El Bar Central*, is the president of San Pedro's *Junta*. Don Julio is a native of San Pedro as was his father. Neither he, nor his father, nor any member of his family, has been a public official. Probably for this reason Don Julio does not dwell upon his own importance in furthering the *Junta*'s aims. He is even able to voice the trite, over-killed phrases of the committee's philosophy in a manner refreshing in its sincerity. He explains, "The mission of the *Junta Comunal* is to help people help themselves. Its overall design is to raise the standard of living and thus to combat the menace of Communism." "Communism," he emphasizes, "flourishes where misery exists, therefore if misery can be abolished through economic improvement, Communism will have no appeal." "For the *Junta* to succeed," he adds, "people in San Pedro have to work together. I am a Conservative and the *alcalde*, who is a board member, is a Liberal. Yet the *Junta* is not political. When a thing is political, one has to fight. When a thing, like the *Junta*, is not political, one needs to cooperate."

The San Pedro committee receives little help from the government, according to Don Julio. San Pedro is small, and the government only listens to the large cities. So the *Junta* has to raise its own money, and it has had some mishaps. The members sponsored a horse race for several Sundays, but attendance disappeared when it became apparent that a white mare could beat all comers. They had a very successful fiesta in the town park. A live band of a guitar, a *bandola* (sixteen string mandolin), and a saxophone provided music for dances that lasted until midnight. However, the next day the *alcalde* and the *personero* (an official responsible for the upkeep of the *municipio*) complained to Don Julio about the condition of the park. They said the damage was so great that the *Junta* could not use it again. The priest would not allow them to use the parish hall, and Don Julio thought it was because the priest wanted to reserve the hall for fiestas that would raise money for the church—perhaps not a high minded aim on the part of the priest but an understandable one in the light of difficulties in raising money in a poor town.

A few months later after this pessimistic account of the committee's affairs, Julio reported better success. A more receptive priest had replaced the stubborn one and not only had lent the hall but had given his personal encouragement as well. The *alcalde* had also become more cooperative. From the money that it had raised the *Junta* was piping water into the houses of the very poor and installing toilets and wash basins in these same houses. It was supplying drugs free of charge and had opened a small store to sell food at low prices. Don Julio was much encouraged.

Work, *Cultura*, and *Los Pobres*

Don Julio's moderate success with the *Junta Comunal* is tempered by his sure knowledge that San Pedro cannot prosper. It is a small town; politicians listen to cities, and then, only during election time. Its people are poor, and they are made poor because of the rapacious, exploitive rich who care only for themselves.

Julio's pessimism, the slight sneer of the mouth, the shrug of the shoulders, is the *sanpedrano* version of what their economic status realistically is. *Sanpedrano* realism states that their town is a backward place, full of poor people who have no *cultura*. Yet not everybody is the same and not every type of work is equal. Some work is male work, some is female; and more importantly, some work brings *cultura*, other types do not.

The work of men is usually outside the home and that of women usually inside. *Sanpedrano* men do not stand on their dignity as much as do men in the affluent, servant rich city homes. Many of them will assist their wives, especially if the job, such as a thorough cleaning, calls for heavy labor. For women the two major, local occupations opened to them outside the home are chicken raising and cigar making. Women, particularly the unmarried, the widowed, and the abandoned, can legitimately work in these jobs without eyebrows being raised. One *sanpedrana* has raised so many eyebrows that no one pays much attention to her anymore: one of the functions present in the cities of Buga and Tuluá but absent in the town of San Pedro is prostitution. This woman became a procuress. Each weekend she brings girls from the neighboring cities to her bar-brothel located near the cemetery. On Sunday evening or Monday morning, after the last client has left, she returns the girls to their permanent residence. With even less regard for society's expectations, she wears heavy slacks instead of dresses and drives her pick-up truck like a man.

The classification of work into male and female is of minor importance compared to the evaluation of it. One type of work demands that a person sweat in the sun. This work is physically exhausing; it brings in little profit, requires no education, and has little *cultura*. This "sun work," as the anthropologist calls it, contrasts with "shade work." Shade work is performed in the cool interior of a factory or an office and demands less of the hauling, pulling, and bending muscles. The work brings a profit and requires education. It not only has *cultura*, but it is a pathway for gaining more.

What is *cultura*? In the small, poor town context of San Pedro, *cultura* includes the possession of the artifacts of an industrial society. It is the ownership of cars, refrigerators, radios, and watches. On a more modest scale, it is the possession of mass produced, plastic-covered furniture, gaudy, sentimental pictures, and all the brassy, highly colored, sweet smelling knickknacks that intellectuals contemptuously label philistine. But *cultura* also means participation in the arts, the reading and writing of poetry and of novels; the appreciation of language and of the great artists, such as Cervantes, Shakespeare, and Valencia; and the study of the great heroes of Colombia, such as Santander, Nariño, but above all, Bolívar, whose mighty feats, unlike those of Washington, are still mystical and inspiring.

Cultura is a goal not achieved by *sanpedranos*. Few of them are cultured in either sense of the word; their poverty forbids them. Yet they attempt to do things that cultured people do. The *alcalde* buys a refrigerator. Seneca writes poems in praise of his mother and saves notable quotations, particularly the "beautiful" ones of his Latin namesake.

The strive for *cultura* forced the anthropologist into the unfamiliar role of teacher of English. At the request of men like Carlos and Ramiro, the anthropologist taught English during the evenings. Despite the handicaps of a teacher whose English was anything but pure and of classes which came after a hard day of work for some and a full day of school for others, men—but not women— teenage girls and boys, and young children came to class after class for two and a half months. Their enthusiasm came out of a desire to appreciate, not English, but a cultured thing, a foreign language.

Work that does not encourage the appreciation of cultured things is work that can only be endured. Sun work in general does not encourage *cultura*, and the lowest type of sun work, according to those not engaged in that work, is picking cotton, a crop produced by several of the valley *haciendas*. One evening Señora Beserra and two of her mature children were idly talking of going to the United States. They were speculating on the money they could make and of the cultured things they could enjoy. The anthropologist recalled how his countrymen treat unskilled foreigners, particularly those with dark skins, and shuddered at the mental image of the proud Señora reduced to spiritual impoverishment. He tried to dampen their enthusiasm, "Yes, there is a lot of money, but jobs for foreigners can be scarce." Groping about in his own background for an example he said, "You could pick cotton." "Pick cotton!" they chorused. "¡Que va! No, señor," the daughter who worked in the cigar factory made clear. "I don't pick cotton. That is the work of the *iguazas*, those people at the level of the bird that lives on the water. It is work without *cultura*."

Not all types of sun work are treated in such a contemptuous manner, even by those who work in the shade. Conversely all shade jobs do not have equal value but are differentiated according to income, power, and *cultura*. The following chart, restricted to agriculture, cigar manufacturing, and the governmental bureaucracy, is a rough approximation of the complexities of *sanpedrano* evaluations.

SUN WORK	SHADE WORK	
Agriculture	Cigar Industry	Municipio Personnel
—	owners	officers
farmer-owners	—	—
—	—	employees
sharecroppers	—	—
—	workers	—
—	—	laborers
laborers	—	—

The most prestigious category of sun work is that filled by the landowning farmers; these in turn are individually ranked according to their success and their use of modern technology. Like the Lozano father, many, but not all, of the moderately success farmers withdraw from the actual farmwork. They turn the work over to their sons, hire laborers, or let out their land to sharecroppers. The most prosperous farmers, such as Gutiérrez, have a standing almost equal to that of the higher *municipio* officers, like Don Hernán, the *alcalde.* Individual sharecroppers and laborers may earn the praise of being a *muy trabajador,* a "hard worker." They are people who not only work hard but whose efforts have also resulted in economic advancement.

Because they are metaphorically in the shade and are people of substance, the larger factory owners are roughly equal to the highest *municipio* official, the *alcalde,* although because of the power of his office, Don Hernán may have slightly higher standing in the eyes of the townsmen. The *municipio* laborers, because of their relatively steady employment, may have a bit more standing than do the agricultural workers, certainly more than cotton pickers—except in the minds of those who pick cotton.

The *antioqueño* mystique intrudes into the sun work–shade work classification and cuts across it. The ethic of the people from Antioquia and Caldas does not permit them the luxury of ignoring work because it is sweaty; it drives them to seek a profit whatever the nature of the labor.

"An *antioqueño* and a native *sanpedrano* were sitting in the park," one illustrative story goes. "It was evening and both were tired after a long day's work. A horseman rode up and offered 10 pesos to the one who would unsaddle his horse and put him out to pasture. The *sanpedrano* looked away, bored. The *antioqueño,* immediately alert, calculated how long it would take him to earn 10 pesos. Satisfied, he grabbed the reins almost before the owner had dismounted. This is why *antioqueños* do not have many front teeth. Once they do go to bed, they are too tired to clean them."

The ethic is not hollow. Of the fifty-six heads of *antioqueño* families in San Pedro a greater percentage are agricultural laborers and a greater percentage are farm-owners than native born *sanpedranos.* The distribution supports the reputation that *antioqueños* will labor in work that others shun and that they will achieve success where others fail.

Some work is male; some is female. One type of work is in the sun and has no *cultura*; another type is in the shade and has *cultura.* Native *sanpedranos* take life as it is; *antioqueños* extract money from it. These are some of the concepts that the townsmen use to catalog and evaluate the economic activity that goes on about them. Additional characterizations—and ones with less anthropological tinkering and thus more directly from the townspeople—are the polar contrasts of *tradicional–moderno, atrasado–progresivo,* and *los pobres–los ricos.* A technique is either traditional or modern, an economy is either backward or progressive, and a person is either poor or rich. These contrasts are not objective pigeon holes, but they are full of meaning about what is best and what is worst. They are not descriptive statements but are normative contrasts.

Tradicional-moderno. Traditional agricultural techniques produce little, they necessitate large amounts of manual labor, and they are not scientific. The farmers that employ such techniques are usually small landowners. A person does not often refer to his own practices as being traditional but uses the term to mildly disparage the actions of others and to label the practitioners of such techniques as ignorant. Modern agricultural techniques are those that yield large quantities, are mechanized, and are scientific; the farmers using such techniques frequently own large acreages. When a person calls his own techniques, and those of others, modern, he is praising them and labeling the users as intelligent.

Atrasado–progresivo. To characterize an economy as backward is to denounce its techniques as traditional and its people as poor. A progressive economy is the economy of a town that is *civilizado* and that produces jobs that maintain life with at least a moderate degree of comfort. People who know San Pedro but who do not live there, almost always refer to it as a backward place. Instead of calling their home backward, the *sanpedranos* say it is not progressive. They are not quite so harsh in their denunciation. Not quite. Notwithstanding the recent technological and economic improvements such as the installation of piped water, the expansion of the tobacco factories, the rapid development of the chicken industry, and the work of the *Junta Comunal,* the people of San Pedro do not conceive of their economy as expanding, of jobs becoming available, or of themselves as being moderately comfortable.

Doña Jaél, the wife of the *personero,* made a typical remark about her town and its people. Upon hearing that the attendance to the English classes had, after two and a half months, dwindled down to a single person, Don Carlos, she caustically observed, "People here get enthusiastic about something new and work at it very hard for a few days, then they give it up. This is the way this town is, and this is why it is not progressive. *Sanpedranos* will not put forth the effort necessary to improve themselves."

The *atrasado–progresivo* contrast is a link between the *tradicional–moderno* and *los pobres–los ricos* ones. An economy of a town is *atrasado* because *tradicional* techniques which produce *los pobres.*

Los pobres–los ricos. *Sanpedranos* think of their town, their fellow citizens, and themselves as being poor. Being poor means no money, no *cultura,* and no power. Beyond these features, the term becomes ambivalent. When he calls himself poor, a *sanpedrano* is pleading for help. To be poor in this sense is to be a worthy recipient of aid. A poor person is a good person. His wife is never like the wives of rich men. "Rich women go from one man to another. In 100 marriages among the rich, there are 101 unfaithful women."

When he calls himself poor, a person entitles himself to help. When he calls other people poor, even fellow townsmen, he is sneering at their condition and scorning at their efforts: "Look at him! See how poor he is. He is ignorant and doesn't have a thing!"

At first glance, the ambivalence of sympathy for one's self and scorn for others seems missing in the concept of *los ricos*. As a class the rich are evil. They exploit the poor. Indeed, they are the reason why poor people exist in Columbia. "The rich don't care for the poor. They have not conscience for Colombia. They run the country to suit themselves." The rich have money and *cultura* because the poor have neither. Both money and *cultura* are limited resources, and the rich have monopolized both. Yet the *sanpedrano* does not spread his distaste for the rich to encompass their activities. The rich are to be despised, for they exploit the poor. *Cultura*, on the other hand, is to be sought after and enjoyed; the advantages of being rich is that one can spend more time in that valuable, pleasurable involvement.

So the meanings associated with the concept of *los ricos* are as inevitably contradictory as those connected with *los pobres*. "I am poor because of the rich class. So I hate the rich. They have denied me money and *cultura*. But I want *cultura*. I want to have money. I want to be rich. Yet I can't. *Los políticos*, the politicians, the conspirators with the rich, prohibit me."

4

The Political Side

THE COLOMBIAN ECONOMIC SYSTEM broadly dictates the economic roles that the *sanpedranos* play. The nation's government and its resident politicians even more precisely delineate their political acts. Viewed politically, San Pedro constitutes the end point of a network that extends through the regional capital of Cali and terminates in Bogotá. The laws and decrees that originate in those two cities stop at San Pedro, and the political parties that the urban elites control claim the loyality of the townspeople.

The *sanpedranos* talk discontentedly about their economic state, but they verbally ravage their national government and its leaders. Colombia in general and the politician in particular are continually hauled across the fire of their scorn. The United States, as a dispenser of cultured things, fares somewhat better, but it too is called to reckoning for its selfish exploitation of poor nations.

The *Municipio*

The administrative apparatus of the Colombian government extends out of the planning rooms of the bureaucrats and eventually comes to rest on the countryside and in the behavior of people. At this minimal, local level the administrative structure mingles with the more ancient, Hispanic tradition of community democracy. The mixture of appointive officialdom and local autonomy produces a geographical and social product unlike any in the United States—the *municipio*. As a geographical expression, the *municipio* consists of a single, relatively large, nucleated center with numerous, smaller, satellite communities. As a social unit, the *municipio* is composed of a *cabecera*, the administrative seat located in the large center, and the *corregimientos*, the satellite settlements and their adjacent territories. The *cabecera* bears the same names as the *municipio*; San Pedro, the town, administrates San Pedro, the *municipio*. The *corregimientos* are miniature editions of the *municipio*. Each *corregimiento* has a micro-center of a few houses, a primary school, a chapel, and one or two stores. The center has the same name as its adjacent territory and is the official residence of the single *corregimiento* official, the police inspector. Appointed by the governor of the *departamento*, the police inspector acts as the *alcalde*'s man on the spot and is charged with the maintenance of law and order.

The town of San Pedro is a social unit only to the extent of being a *cabecera*, as being the official residence of the *municipio* officials. Although these officials work in their town offices, their responsibilities are limited not by town boundaries but by *municipio* ones. The town is not an administrative entity in itself. There is no mayor of the town, but only a *municipio alcalde*.

The small, compact state of the *municipio* is a micro-copy of the larger *departamento* and national governments. The executive, legislative, and judicial branches are squeezed into the offices of the *alcaldía*, the council, and the judiciary. The executive, the *alcaldía*, is the cutting edge of local government, and the *alcalde*, Don Hernán, is an important man in town, perhaps as important as the priest. The president of the Republic appoints the government of the *Departamento del Valle*; the governor appoints the *alcalde* of San Pedro. The governor selects the *alcalde* from a list presented to him by the local directorate of the majority political party. In San Pedro this is the Liberal party. Don Hernán says that unlike some *municipios* where the majority party bluntly ignores the minority, the Liberals of San Pedro consult with the much smaller number of Conservatives about its list of possible appointees for the *alcalde* office. In the spirit of the National Front coalition, the two local parties agree on the best possible candidate.

The appointment of *alcalde* is normally for a year, but Don Hernán, who has been *alcalde* for fifteen months and likes the position, ruefully points out there is little security in the position. The governor can recall the appointment at any time, and the people of the *municipio* can petition for his removal. So Don Hernán sits gingerly in his chair.

He performs a broad array of duties. He administers the laws of the *departamento*. Working with the *municipio* judge, he arbitrates such minor disputes as those of water and property rights. As head of the *corregimiento* inspectors and of the *municipio* police force, he is a type of police chief-sheriff-judge, and in this capacity he makes arrests and imposes small fines. To carry out the work of the *municipio*, he notifies the council that he needs additional personnel, and from the list the council sends him, he selects a suitable man.

Perhaps Don Hernán's most important job is to let the government in Cali know the needs of his people, that his *municipio* needs roads into the mountains and that the town must have secondary schools to avoid the expense of sending the children to Buga or to Tuluá. In expressing these needs, Don Hernán self-consciously adopts the posture of a father looking after his children. He explains that he is like a family head demanding order and harmony in his household. The ordinary person is one without influence and without protection against the rapacious politicians. For his children's sake, Don Hernán puts on his armor of wisdom and lays on his influence among the bureaucratic dragons in Cali.

The popular, local autonomous side of the community is the *municipio* council. *Sanpedranos* elect eight men every two years from a slate of candidates

The alcaldía *and the* alcalde.

selected by the local directorates. In close conformity with the National Front coalition, membership in the council is equally divided between Liberals and Conservatives. The councilmen do not necessarily have to live in San Pedro. More important than residence are their qualifications as people with connections in Cali. The ideal councilman is one who knows the needs of San Pedro and who can exert influence in the offices of the *departamento*.

The council meets twice each year to discuss and to act upon *municipio* problems. The day-to-day work of the council is conducted by the council appointees, the *personero* and the treasurer. The *personero* is charged with the upkeep of the *municipio*. The council authorizes him to buy new equipment, such as horses, saddles, and tools, and to let out contracts for work on the public buildings and schools. In San Pedro the *personero* is a man of some stature and people call him the foreman of the *municipio*. The treasurer's main task is to collect local taxes at a rate fixed by the council. The taxes come from many sources, from property, businesses, cattle butchered in the *municipio*, cattle brought in from other areas, and so on. Despite the variety of sources, the budget of the *municipio* depends heavily upon the government in Cali.

The minister of justice in Bogotá names the members of the superior court of the Buga judicial district. The Buga court appoints the *municipio* judge of San Pedro. The judge must belong to the majority political party, to the same party as the *alcalde*, with whom he works closely. Don Hector is the prototype of a small town official. His essential friendliness mediates his pride in being an official and cushions his back slapping attitude toward his cronies. He has learned the ins and outs of small town officialdom from twenty-eight years of experience. During these years he has been one or more times the assistant of the *alcalde*, the assistant of the judge, *alcalde*, and judge in towns all through out the Valle. Don Hector says that he could have been *alcalde* this time around in San Pedro, but he prefers the judgeship. It carries more security, and according to Don Hector, it occupies a higher category. However, no sooner than he made these remarks, the superior court moved Don Hector on to Yotoco and replaced him with a young, university trained man.

Don Hector presides over both civil and criminal matters. He settles land disputes, inheritance fights, and matrimonial estrangements. He also judges cases of thefts involving small sums. He can extract fines and sentence short jail terms. With the help of physicians he decides the cause of death, and on the request of the *alcalde*, he holds hearings on the conduct of *municipio* officials. Small wonder his office is called The Promiscuous County Court.

In addition to the *municipio* government, there are a few other offices in the town, such as the *departamento* tax assessor and the criminal court newly established to combat *violencia*.

Political Parties

In Colombia and in San Pedro, as is true of all modern governmental systems, holding an administrative office means membership in a political party. Whether the office is an appointive one, such as *alcalde*, or an elective one, such as councilman, candidates must first pass through the screen of the party apparatus. The "law of parity," put together by the party elites in Bogotá and ratified by the plebiscite in 1957, further determines who will hold what office. The parity ruling dictates that in San Pedro, both the *alcalde* and the *municipio* judge must belong to the majority party, the council must be divided equally, and the council appointees—the *personero* and the treasurer—must belong to opposite parties. Finally, all assistants, *secretarios*, are to be of the party opposite to that of their superiors. The resulting distribution of this complicated scheme is the *alcalde*, the judge, four councilmen, and the treasurer are Liberals; the *personero*, four councilmen, and the *secretarios* of the *alcalde*, of the judge, and of the treasurer are Conservatives.

The two traditional parties extended beyond the mere qualifications for local office holding and penetrate deeply into the feelings of the townspeople. Being a Conservative or being a Liberal is included in the small list of things that really matter. The intense identification with an elite controlled political party is, to the small-town North American, one of San Pedro's most familiar paradoxes. At this local level party ideological differences become even more blurred than they are in the rarified air of the party intellectual. Yet the feelings that to be a Liberal or a Conservative is to be on the side of truth and justice are more sincere, and more appreciated in San Pedro than in the sophisticated skepticism of the party elites.

As is the case of Mainstreet, the San Pedro version of political parties is best summed up as a collection of "hereditary hatreds" (coined by Miguel Antonio Caro, Dix:211). Although local Liberals, like Chucho and Seneca, make the approved criticism of priests as businessmen, their anti-clerical feelings seem to well-up from a source different from Liberal party ideology. They and the Conservatives, such as the *personero* and the high school principal, frequently pronounce that party politicians, be they Liberal or Conservative, are equally corrupt. Yet along with Don Julio César of the *Junta Comunal*, when a thing is political, they are ready for battle. Rather than stemming from ideological commitment, the intensity of party feeling comes from one's parents. Party affiliation is a matter of inheritance rather than one of calculation based on individual self-interest.

The inheritance of party membership is graphically displayed in the distribution of party membership in the Cauca Valley. *Sanpedranos* say, and voting records support them, that Conservatives live in the western mountains of the valley and Liberals live in the eastern ranges. On the valley floor and in San Pedro, because of the movement of people, both parties are present. The distribution cuts across such categories as rural-urban, plantation worker-*haciendo* owner, and small town-large city, and thus seems to be primarily a result of familial traditions.

The inheritance of party membership does not mean slavish adherence to party wishes. The vote of San Pedro in the presidential elections of 1962 attest to the people's independence. In that year, the second trial for the National Front, the orthodox Conservatives and Liberals put forth the Conservative, Guillermo León Valencia. In accordance with the agreement of 1957, the country, having had a Liberal, Lleras Camargo, as president, was now due a Conservative. However, a Liberal faction could not lay down in the same bed with the Conservatives. So the faction offered Lopez Michelson, son of the famous president Alfonso Lopez for the high office, even though, because of the 1957 agreement, he could not legally hold office. The majority of the Liberals of the San Pedro *municipio* went against the directive of their party leaders and voted for Lopez. The National Front candidate received only 431 votes, primarily from the Conservatives—although even a few of the Conservatives rebelled and voted for *their* party's splinter faction led by Jorge Leyva—and from the Liberals holding *municipio* offices. Lopez received a whopping 1320.

Neither does the inheritance of party membership mean that the party escapes the fire of *sanpedrano* denunciation. Those that run the party and those that guide the country are *los políticos*, the politicians. *Político* is a dirty word in San Pedro; it rivales *el rico* for top place in the large inventory of dispicable things. *Políticos* are selfish and deceitful. During their campaigns for office, they make sweeping commitments, but when elected they rarely carry through even a fraction of what they promised. "The governor said he would come to San Pedro and see to our needs. Well, we are waiting," said Don Guido. "But he probably won't come. We are a small, poor town." Ramiro is active in local politics and belongs to the *municipio* council, but typically, his feelings about being a Conservative do not hinder him for characterizing all *políticos* as parasitic exploiters. He disgustedly concluded, "Neither the Liberal party nor my own party is doing anything about land reform. They don't care."

The *sanpedranos* scorch the world of *políticos* and parties with their volcanic blasts, which are simultaneously both disturbing in their ferocity and boring in their repetition. Yet while they catalog sin after sin of *los políticos*, they become strangely quiet and admiring when they think about particular leaders. The Liberals still recall the great popular leader, Jorge Gaitán, some fourteen years after his death. They also speak admiringly of Lleras Camargo. "He is a person of *cultura*," Chucho explained. "He can read English, German, and French. Although he didn't finish high school and was poor, he is very intelligent." Then Chucho gave his ultimate endorsement, "He is a man I respect." Laureano Gómez, the aristocrat of Hispanic virtue, also finds admirers in San Pedro, but the dictator, Rojas Pinilla was, in 1962–1963, an all but forgotten man.

The *sanpedranos* also allow local officials to escape from their verbal clubbing of the political world. Perhaps in the distant, isolated communities in the mountains, the *alcalde*, the judge, and the *municipio* council receive their share of denunciations, but in the town, people are nonchalant about the local branch of the nation's government, neither demeaning nor praising the officials.

Between themselves and a particular national leader or between the townspeople and *municipio* officials, the *sanpedranos* seem to have constructed a special, personal tie. The tie with national persons springs from the *sanpedrano*'s own creative urge to seek a long distant, but intimate social connection. His tie with the local officials requires less personal creativity. The *municipio* government is not isolated off in the multistoried edifices of Cali or in the monumental structures of Bogotá but is housed in friendly, informal buildings that the townsman sees everytime he crosses the plaza. In the pursuit of his everyday business the townsman sees the *alcalde*, the judge, or one of the councilmen and appreciates that the work they do is in the shade and is full of *cultura*. Finally and brutally, twenty-six heads of *sanpedrano* families receive their income from the local government and in an environment characterized by a scarcity of jobs, they, their wives, and their children can hardly afford the luxury of verbal destruction.

"Nos Duele Colombia"

Colombian author and university professor Eduardo Santa wrote a small essay on Colombian political society. Disturbed by national events, he titled his book *Nos Duele Colombia*. There is no better label to attach to the feelings expressed by the *sanpedranos* about their country than the English translation, "Colombia Pains Us."

When a person "pains" another in American English he is either being an aggravating bore, as in "You're a big pain," or he is the source of deep mental torment, as the "The pain that you caused me." Colombia "pains" the people of San Pedro in both ways. The pain of the *los políticos* and their co-conspirators, *los ricos,* is largely the wearily aggravating type. *Políticos* bore the townspeople with their promises which in local view are both grandiose and empty. The whole complex of national bureaucracy and elite maneuverings sits on their minds like a great, gigantic nuisance. But Colombia also produces the deeper pain of mental anguish. It does this in the way that all nations do, through producing a series of inevitable contradictions which its citizens try hopelessly to resolve.

Being a Liberal to a *sanpedrano* means that he is ready to fight a Conservative, but it also means to be constantly led astray by *políticos* scheming anonymously in Cali and Bogotá. Being a Colombian is a proud thing. It means to be a direct descendant of the great heroes of the past, to be part of Bolívar, father of the Republic, and of Belalcázar, conquistador of the Cauca Valley. It means to be part of Columbus, the man who began it all, and the man whom no off-spring of northern Europe can admire with the same intensity that the descendants of Ferdinand and Isabella can. Being Colombian means speaking the purest Spanish, producing the best coffee, and having the most beautiful women. But being Colombian also means fearing the neighbors' eyes, withdrawing turtlelike into the house when night falls, and worst of all, living amidst the *violencia.*

La violencia began in 1948 with the assassination of Jorge Gaitán and the social explosion in Bogotá. Since that time it has moved across the countryside at different rates and under different guises. The first wave of 1948–1953 engulfed most of the country and peaked in the Andean region of the Central and Western Cordillera and again in the flat, cattle country of the Llanos. According to Liberals, this wave began when the Conservatives, who were then in power and who claimed at least the silent consent of Laureano Gómez, started persecuting the Liberals. With little restraint from their own leaders, the Liberals retaliated, and the *violencia* approximated an undeclared civil war.

Rojas Pinilla was at first successful in pacifying the country but toward the end of his administration acts of violence increased. The second wave peaked within the more narrow confines of Tolima, Caldas, and Valle and was particularly strong from 1955 to 1958. Until 1963 the acts of organized *violencia* still exploded in the mountainous areas of the three *departamentos* and particularly in Tolima. Since 1963 a steady decline has occurred.

The second episode of *violencia,* particularly during 1962–1963, was neither openly nor, presumably, silently sanctioned by the national elite. The leaders of the undeclared civil war were being replaced by people who grew up among the acts of violence and who consequently conceived of *violencia* as a way of life and as an effective means of obtaining both material goods and emotional satisfaction. In harmony with the rhythm of cold war dialectics, both North Americans and Colombians saw Communists—Russian, Cuban, or Colombian—playing their nefarious part, but at least during 1962–1963 Communism seemed at most to be at the fringe of *violencia* rather than its main driving force.

Estimations of the number of people killed during both waves range from 100,000 to 200,000. If the last figure is true, then Colombia lost a greater proportion of its population than did the United States in World War I, World War II, and the Korean War combined.

In 1962, a minimum definition of *violencia* is that it is the acts of robbery, murder, and mutilation which are performed by groups organized in a pseudo-military fashion. What makes *violencia* killing distinctive from simple murder are the stereotyped mutilations. In a manner analogous to the butchering of cattle, the mutilations are grouped into "*cortes*" or "cuts." The most well known are the *corte de franela* (the flannel cut), in which the victim's head is severed at the neck of his undergarment; the *corte de corbata* (the necktie cut), where the throat and the floor of the mouth are sliced and the tongue pulled back through the throat slit forming a "necktie," and the *corte de canoa* (the canoe cut), in which the stomach and chest are laid open and the internal organs scooped out to form a "canoe" out of the body.

For a period the Cali press accompanied their front page treatment of *violencia* with large photographs of the victims. This type of journalism, whatever its other effects, must have considerably shortened the time spent browsing the newspaper at breakfast, for eggs and decapitated *campesinos* do not mix.

The various *violencia* bands are under the leadership of "captains" who frequently adopt a nickname, such as the famous *Capitán Chispas* (Captain Sparks) and the less well known *Capitán Sangrenegra* (Captain Blackblood) and *Capitán Tarzán* (Captain Tarzan). The analogy between these "captains" and the various outlaw bands operating during and immediately after the North American Civil War is tempting but incomplete. For while Quantrill's Raiders, the James Boys, and the Younger Brothers were armed with revolvers, Captain Chispas shoots with a machine gun. Furthermore, either because the *violencia* acts are contemporary or the circumstance is different, the romantic legend of Jessie James robbing from the rich to give to the poor is only weakly present in the San Pedro accounts. The local Liberals occasionally explain that Chispas began his career in retaliation against the Conservatives who drove his family from their home and burned their house. So, the Liberals say, there is some justification for his acts. Even they, however, attribute the slaughter of innocent peasants to Chispas and condemn the present wave of *violencia* as out and out banditry. A more contemporary similiarity is the act of a certain Colombian beauty queen. She, in a style that even the most publicity conscious Hollywood star would envy, offered to go into the mountains and personally talk Chispas into surrendering. The Cali papers, while courteously noting her genuine qualifications as a beautiful, gentle woman, urged that her offer not be accepted. It was not.

Even the earlier, more widespread wave of *violencia* never penetrated into the town of San Pedro. Feelings between the Liberals and the Conservatives became taut with tension when the victims of the violence in the mountains came to town to find shelter in the Church. But the small town virtues of harmony and tranquility endured. The most notable incident occurred one dark night when two Conservatives stole the statue of a Liberal benefactor from the plaza park.

The townspeople of different political parties still walk gingerly around each other, suddenly rushing together to embrace with loud proclamations of peace and friendship, then retiring once more apart, each muttering under his breath, "Atheistic Liberal;" "Conservative Brute." In the mountains people still kill each other, not as often, but just as effectively. Shortly before Christmas, Seneca accompanied the *alcalde* into the mountains to bring down a woman killed by bandits. He was full of disgust for the woman had been dead for eight days, and she was very green and very smelly. In the spring Don Hernán received news of more trouble. Despite the *alcalde*'s earlier warnings, a small group of Liberal men crossed through a pocket of Conservative territory on their way down the mountains to Tuluá. The Conservatives caught them and killed them. On hearing the account, one townsman said that the police of Tuluá would do little for they were mostly Conservatives. Another Liberal added that recently a squad of Conservative soldiers found a teenage boy they thought guilty of a certain act. They exclaimed how dirty he was and threw him into a river. As he crawled out, the boy complained that he was cold. "You're cold, are you?" the corporal in charge sneered. "Then let's warm you." They poured kerosene on the boy and set him afire. Somehow the boy survived and is now in the Buga Hospital. Don Hernán wearily commented that if the story is true, he is going to have to ride up to the boy's community and try to convince the people that the soldiers will be punished. Unless he succeeds, the people are sure to join with the bandits and start killing soldiers, and not necessarily the guilty ones.

The events that happen in the mountains are interpreted through the political biases of the *sanpedranos*. When the final account emerges, its validity is not to be found in its objectivity but in its expression of political antagonism. Notwithstanding the charges that *los políticos* beguile the poor with hollow ideological statements, party affiliation is one of the primeval guides in *sanpedrano* life. Party loyalty structures the events of *violencia* and makes them meaningful. The story that best reflects the role of party commitment in the local interpretation of *violencia* is Seneca's account of what happened to the *alcalde* when they went on another trip into the mountains. "It was raining hard," Seneca began, "and both of us were slunked down in the saddles with our hats pulled down and the collars of our raincoats turned up. A group of bandits, Liberal ones, suddenly appeared. Before we could say a word, they began shooting. The *alcalde* shouted at them, 'Don't shoot! I'm Don Hernán, the Liberal *alcalde* of San Pedro!' When they heard him, the bandits immediately stopped. They were embarrassed and quickly apologized. Don Hernán was lightly wounded and they gave him money to pay for his doctor bill."

The *sanpedranos* have additional explanations for *la violencia: Los ricos*, always greedy and wanting more land, hire bandits to kill off and drive away the small farmer. Land prices fall and *los ricos*, in the fashion of the cattle-barons of the Old West, grab the land at half its value. The reason why bandits mutilate their victims is their lack of *cultura*. These bandits are ignorant and are like beasts. Once the townsman has exhausted the basic interpretations of party vengeance, the exploitive rich, and the lack of *cultura*, he shrugs off the remaining acts of *violencia* as simple robbery.

The United States

One great difference divides the people of San Pedro and their small town counterparts in the United States. The *sanpedranos* talk much more about the

United States. Accurately reflecting the structural relation between the United States and Colombia, a constantly shifting relation between primary producer and hinterland, the comments of the townspeople are both caustic and admiring.

If their own nation "pains" the townspeople, the United States pesters them. "The United States sends cigarettes to Colombia. They can't sell them in their own country because they cause cancer, so they send them here." explained Pedro. Don Carlos observed, when the fire engines brought water from Tuluá to carry San Pedro through a drought and a rupture in the water line, "The climate is much drier these days than when I was a kid. Some people say, and they may be right, that the United States and other countries are changing the weather with the testing of the atomic bombs." "It is true, isn't it, *mister*," stated Doña Leonor, "that the physicians in the United States, and also I believe in Russia, kill deformed children."

Shortly after New Year's there was a protest in Cali against the rising cost of living. Seneca said that this was the fault of the United States. "Each president of Colombia has to pay more and more money to the United States because of the North American loans. So the presidents have to raise taxes on importations." Ninivé was more direct, "The United States has made the dollar more dear. It does this in order to exploit Colombia."

As soon as they make these criticisms, the townsmen turn to complimenting the United States. It is a dispenser of cultured things. The best clothes, the most pleasing household articles, and the most cultured movies come from North America. But it was President Kennedy who called forth their deepest admiration. When Russia and the United States met eyeball to eyeball in the Caribbean, the *sanpedranos* enthusiastically supported Kennedy and followed him to greatness. It was not the correctness of the United States' position that won their approval, but rather it was the images they had of Kennedy, his youth, his vitality, his successes, his Catholicism, but most of all, his heroism, that drew them. The United States, Russia, and the cold war was one thing; John Kennedy was another.

5

The Religious Side

As CATHOLICS, the *sanpedranos* are the behavioral termini, the final testing ground, of an international cultural system that antedates the Republic by some 1800 years. The people, conscious of their participation in this massive enterprise, honor the founding of their religion with an energy which far exceeds that dissipated on the day their nation was born. Only school children and governmental officials observe the birth of Colombia. Other people go about their work. Chucho opens and closes the doors of his factory at the same hours. Simeón disappears into his chicken houses. Anibal searches for firewood. Doña Leonor goes to shop in Tuluá. Don Julio does a reasonably good business at *El Bar Central*, but the turnover is nothing compared to a Saturday afternoon, not to mention a Sunday.

The townspeople are born citizens of Colombia. They are also, almost without exception, born Catholics. Catholicism is not something to be pursued as if it might be out of reach; it is what one has, nearly in the same way that one has two legs, a mother, sisters, or brothers.

No other religion successfully competes for the people's attention. Whatever Indian heritage they may once have had has long since dissolved into scattered odds and ends. The more recent potential competitor, Protestantism, is frozen to its North American matrix. Protestantism is un-Colombian to the *sanpedranos* in the same way that Catholicism is un-American to the hill towns in the southern United States. The best that Protestanism can do in San Pedro is to claim eight or so people who now and then slip back to the Mother Church.

The *sanpedranos* are orthodox, but not perfect, Catholics. They frequently confuse the historic and mythic figures of their faith. Some say things that would make a theological purist shudder; but then the purist does not have to extract meaning from the drab facts of ordinary, small town existence. Whatever its character, the Catholicism of the townspeople is all they have and is all the religion they want. In this sense, their faith is as orthodox as that of the Pope.

The Church as a Social Body

Nationally, the church is the most powerful, single organization in Colombia. Its strength derives from being the institution which most fully embodies the values of traditional Colombian society. It encompasses all social classes and cuts across political party lines, but its power rests on the ties between the clergy and the secular elite. The church has its own educational system and owns the majority of the country's secondary schools. It exercises considerable influence on secular training, and instruction in its catechism is required in all public schools. Church charities are the traditional means of redistributing the national wealth, and they continue to receive governmental support. The government nearly always includes a church official in its commissions on agrarian reform and on *violencia*, and any public ceremony requires at least one priest in attendance.

Despite the anticlerical stance of the Liberal party, a posture often more ritualistic than effective, the church's power has endured. Indeed, the coalition of the two parties may have brought about a closer alliance between the church and the governing elite. Part of the agreement that the Liberal party made with the Conservatives called for the Liberals to recognize that the church officially has a "favorite status." The minority radical wing of the Liberal party has seized upon the issue in their attempt to find a viable political niche and has become increasingly critical of the church establishment. Likewise, those Conservatives who have protested against the National Front coalition have alienated themselves from the church through their persecution of the Liberals during the first stage of the *violencia*. Thus, the enemies of the church, the splinter Liberals and Conservatives, are also the enemies of the governing National Front (Dix:311–313).

Locally, the church's minimal ecclesiastical unit, the parish, coincides with the *municipio*. Just as San Pedro town is the *cabecera* of the secular *municipio*, so also it is the focus of religious activities. All the principal holy days are celebrated in the town church, and all the business of the parish, such as birth registration, baptism, and marriage, are the responsibilities of the town priest and the church *junta*. Away from the town each of the small centers of the *corregimientos* has, or tries to build, its own church. On alternating Sundays and after the mass in town, the priest goes out from his official residence in the town to conduct services in these small churches.

The priest is assisted by parish *junta*. In its periodic meetings in the parish hall located next door to the priest's residence, the *junta* reviews the parish budget and advises the priest on the material, moral, and religious state of the parishioners. In addition to the parish *junta*, each church in the rural areas has its own *junta* which attempts to maintain the affairs of its church during the priest's absences.

The bishop of the Palmira diocese appoints the San Pedro priest, and the bishop can reappoint him to another parish at any time. The parishioners, either through the parish *junta* or outside it, can petition the bishop to remove or to retain the current priest. So, like the *alcalde* and the *municipio* judge, the priest has no tenure, and he also frequently moves from parish to parish.

The church and the priest.

Father Restrepo came into San Pedro with an eagerness and warmth that his predecessor thought inappropriate. Perhaps because he had had his fill of San Pedro, the predecessor made caustic comments about the ignorance of the people and their lack of *cultura*. He saw the *junta comunal* as a competitor for the limited resources of the town and gave it little support. Father Restrepo, on the other hand, sees his job as extending beyond the mass and the confession and into the area of community improvement. He encourages the *junta comunal* and hopes that the church will push for a strong agrarian reform movement. He wants people to get married but agrees that a few couples live honorable lives without the rites. He condemns adultery, is strongly anti-Communist, and does not care for Protestantism. His Sundays begin with an early morning announcement over the loudspeaker. (His fondness of the loudspeaker is almost an addiction.) He reminds people that today is Sunday, that they should come to mass, and that they should help repair the cemetery walls. After the eight o'clock mass in town, he hurries off to the outlying communities and then quickly returns back to his main church to prepare for the sparsely attended evening mass. During the week he goes to the schools to assist the students in their religious instruction. He is trying to hold adult classes in religion but pragmatically realizes that it is difficult for people to take time off from their work to attend. His skin is a deep brown; he talks quickly and frequently, but at the same time he is shy. He is not above rushing up to the billiard table in *El Bar Central*, mixing the balls under the stunned eyes of the players, and then rushing out, laughing at the confusion he has caused. Encountering him in the street is somewhat disconcerting. He hurls himself at you, words piling out of his mouth, his eyes turned away, his hands picking at his loose, black garment, and is gone before you have time to fully comprehend, much less acknowledge, what he had said. No intellectual, he relaxes over Bishop Fulton Sheen. He is the priest of a small town and is a good small town priest.

The religious societies, in addition to the church *junta*, provide a means for the laity to participate in church affairs. Ideally, there is a "brotherhood," a *hermandad*, for each age group and sex. However, only the one for male adults, the Nocturnal Worshippers, and the one for female adults, the Society of the Sacred Heart of Jesus, have functioned effectively. Even the Nocturnal Worshippers have become defunct because the men, afraid of *violencia* and thievery, refuse to leave their homes for the nightly meetings. When working, these two organizations not only engage in religious activities but are also mutual aid groups: for example, if a member is sick, the organization supposedly pays his medical expenses.

Religious training in school attempts to organize the more diffused, yet more meaningful, instruction that the child receives from his parents. The training, from which children of other beliefs are excused, comes directly from the catechism. The teacher asks the question, "Who is God, Our Lord?" The students chorus from memory, "God, Our Lord, is a Being infinitely good, wise, powerful, just, the beginning and the end of all things."

A good knowledge of religion is credited to those who can repeat the catechism. Adults, particularly men, answer a question on religion by attempting to recall the catechism. When they can no longer pull the answer out of their memory, they conclude they do not know much about religion. Chucho, who likes to talk about Catholicism, remarked, "I have a son of five who understands a lot, but usually it is not until seven that a child has the rudiments of the faith. By then he knows to cross himself and to say his prayers. When he is ten, a boy usually knows more about religion than he ever will. By the time he is twenty, his knowledge is fading. Grown men like me, because we don't practice it, forget a great deal." Chucho was in an argument with another man on the question of how many Johns there were. Chucho won because he convinced his audience that John, the Baptist, and John, the Beloved Disciple, were the same person.

The symmetry between church and state, between parish and *municipio*, between priest and *alcalde,* is expressed most vividly in a rite that terminates the mass held on particularly important days. Following communion, the priest returns the host to the monstrance. The monstrance, colored a bright gold, is nearly 3 feet high and consists of a short stand and a large circle formed by small bars radiating, sunlike, from the center. The center has a glass door which opens into a small container, and it is in here that the host is placed. The priest takes the monstrance down from its position above the altar, and with the object carefully held immediately in front of his face, he moves under a canopy of red cloth and gold tassels. The canopy is supported by poles which are held erect by six men.

At the front of the procession is a boy grasping a pole with a small cross on the top. Behind him are several men carrying candles and dressed in freshly ironed shirts and pants. Several of them are without shoes. The *alcalde*, standing a few paces behind the men and well-dressed in a suit and tie, carries a red standard upon which is inscribed the golden monstrance. The assistant priest walks by his side and following them is the altar boy swinging an incense burner. Close behind the altar boy come the canopy and the priest.

Once formed, the procession moves slowly around the church; its speed is determined by the narrow aisle as much as by the holiness of the occasion. The ordinary rumble of the congregation stops, and one can hear the soft murmur of the priest's chant. Even the men in the congregation follow the procession with their eyes as they remain on their knees in worship. After the procession has circled the church, the priest replaces the monstrance and ends the mass.

The highly visible presence of the Catholic Church on the natural and social landscape of Colombia, the church's close ties with the ruling elite, its influence in the schools, and its rituals that ceremonially bind *alcalde* to priest, all jar against the anticlericalism of many *sanpedranos*. People like Seneca and Chucho rarely go to church. In not so cautious a voice they pelt the priests with charges of commercialism.

"Why, the priests are like business men," Seneca knowingly smirked. "They sell the rites of baptism and marriage in the same way that a storekeeper sells pots and pans."

It is standard Liberal doctrine to be against the priestly establishment, but Seneca is not simply repeating the party line. "I'm a good Catholic," he emphatically asserts. "Do you know why? I'm a good Catholic because I believe in God and the Virgin. Our Lord said, 'It is faith that is valuable.' If I have faith, I have that part of religion that is worth the most. People that go to mass frequently do not have faith. At times, the church is a torment. Women that go, go only to gossip about each other and to criticize each other about their dresses and moral habits. But I have faith. I say my prayers. Just because I don't go to church doesn't mean I don't believe. I believe a lot. And I go now and again. I like to hear the mass of the dead, and particularly I like to hear the Gloria sung on Saturday of Holy Week. The Gloria is very beautiful."

Beliefs

The massive ecclesiastical and theological edifice of the Catholic Church, an edifice built from the sediments laid down by centuries of historical meanderings and crisscrossed by intricate solutions to the Christian paradox of a three-in-one God, houses the townspeople of San Pedro. Searching through the labyrinth of dogma for something meaningful to them, as individuals living ordinary lives in a common Colombian town, they have personalized Catholicism into two basic concepts. One is faith. "Our Lord said, 'It is faith that is valuable' " appears in every discussion about religion. Faith is not an attribute bestowed by an outsider, not by God and certainly not by the priest, but it is the possession of a person. It is almost an entity; each person has his own faith, he can bring it forth and intensify it. Faith has value, in the sense of money, but it cannot be depleted; it cannot be mechanically and instrumentally spent to bring favors, for it is not a magical power used to coerce the gods. Rather, faith is the means through which a person establishes a social relation with the supernatural. With faith a person can bypass the priest, the mass, the whole edifice of Catholicism, and reach out directly to God, the Virgin, or the saints.

The second basic conceptual process is the individualization of the supernatural. Out of the array of mythical beings, the townsman picks out one and, through faith, creates an intimate and non-revokable relation.

"I don't know much about the saints," Chucho replied to a question about which saints are the most important. "But it depends on the faith of each person. Some people like this saint; others like that one. I, myself, have faith in the Virgin of Carmen. In Colombia, and especially among men, the greatest faith is in the Virgin of Carmen. To me, she is far more important than the saints."

"Of course," he continued, "everyone has faith in the Virgin Mary. To be a Christian is to have faith in God and in the Holy Virgin. The Virgin is one, the Virgin Mary, the Mother of God. Every Catholic understands this. But the Virgin has revealed herself at different times and at different places. People call these personages different names. For example, The Virgin of Carmen appeared on a hill called Carmel, so she is called Carmen.

"The Virgin of Carmen can perform miracles in every sphere of life. Some people say that each saint has his own thing. Saint Anthony, for example, is good for people in love. Maybe Saint Anthony can do other things as well. Like I said, I don't know much about saints. But I do know that the Virgin of Carmen is good for everything. A person may suffer from a serious illness or from a moral pain. He may need economic help. Whatever it is, he can ask the Virgin of Carmen to help him. She is capable of answering all of his requests. Naturally he must have faith, or she won't respond.

"Let me give you an example. This happened to a friend of mine and I know that it is true. This man took a load of cigars to Cali to sell them. So that he could earn more money, he decided not to pay the governmental tax. He was going to smuggle them to his buyer. Just before he arrived at the buyer's place, the police stopped him. When he saw them coming, he knew what they were after. He said, '*Virgencita del Carmen*, Sweet Virgin of mine, help me.' The police searched his truck, but they did not discover the contraband cigars. The Virgin of Carmen had protected him from the police, just as she had protected me, and just as she will protect anyone who has faith."

"My faith is also in the Virgin of Carmen," agreed the *personero*. "Of course she is not more important than Our Lord, Jesus Christ. But you know, the matter is like a family. The father is the most important person in the family, but the mother loves her children. When children want something from their father, they go to their mother. Because she loves them, she helps them to get what they want from the father. So the Virgin, because she loves her children, will go to Our Lord with their requests."

Seneca claims devotion to the Virgin of Carmen, but his relationship lacks the intensity of the older men. He still remembers from his school days that God assigns each person a guardian angel, and he continues to pray to his own angel. "When you go into the wilds of the mountains, or just before you go to sleep, you pray, 'Saint Angel, who guards me. Sweet companion of mine. Don't leave me, not in the night, nor in the day. Stay until I am in peace with the angels of heaven, with Jesus, Joseph, and Mary.'

"If we honor the guardian angel and put ourselves under his protection, he will keep us from temptation and will save us from injury. Let's say there is a bus wreck. Nineteen of the twenty people die. Why did that one person live? Because his guardian angel protected him. What happened to the guardian angels of the other nineteen? Well, the luck of one is not the luck of another. Besides, before the wreck, their guardian angels had saved them from other accidents."

"*Mister*, I thought sure someone here had stolen your cat," Doña Leonor said to the anthropologist. "I said that to *la mister*, your wife, when she said that Rosita was gone. I'm glad that Rosita has come back. Last night, my daughter and I lit candles and prayed to the Virgin for help." "I prayed too," her youngest daughter chimed in. So had *la mister*.

"I pray to the saints as well," explained Doña Leonor on another occasion. "For example, Saint Rock is very good for curing. He is the lawyer of the sick. If you are ill, then you can make a promise that if Saint Rock cures you, then you will honor him in some way. Light a candle, go to a mass, say the rosary so many times, things like that. He, one of the other saints, or the Virgin could cure you without you making the promise, but it is better, it is more correct, more formal, to make the promise. Of course, if he doesn't answer, then there is no need to complete your promise."

"Yes, it is true that the saints can cure," agreed Seneca. "You usually try them after everything else has failed. But making a promise, no matter how grand it may be, no matter if you promise to walk on your knees from the church entrance to the altar, will be worth nothing, unless you have faith. 'It is faith that is valuable.'

"People who lack faith are those who punish the saints when they do not answer. People such as herbalists, witches, and prostitutes sometimes turn their saint upside down. If they are really angry at the saint, they will throw it outside or put it in water. Girls abuse their saint when he refuses to make boys fall in love with them. They will turn the saint upside down and light a candle under it, or they may do the same thing with a picture of their boyfriend. These are bad actions. It is faith that matters. You have to ask and ask. I don't go to church, but it is bad to abuse the saints."

The Devil in San Pedro, as in so many other Christian towns, has devolved from his position as evil incarnate to a vaguely amusing creature used to reinforce parental authority. "They say that the Devil can make you harm another person," commented Doña Leonor. "This is a very old belief and frankly, I don't believe in it or in the Devil." Her eight year old grandson was trying to get at the truth about the Devil. Puzzled he asked, "But where does he live?" His mother, smiling slightly, replied, "Well, he lives in the wild places and in the bottom of lakes." "What does he do?" persisted her son. "He carries off bad children," she answered. "Oh," uttered the boy.

The townsman of San Pedro makes meaningful the system of Catholic beliefs through the incorporation of the concept of faith and through the creation of a personal relation between himself and a concrete manifestation of the church's supernatural realm. In doing so he all but ignores other manifestations and relegates others, such as the Devil, to minor positions. The concept of faith and the process of individualization are the basic features of his belief system. He is equally selective in his evaluation of the Catholic system of creeds. Certain statements in the Ten Commandments, the Beatitudes, and the Commandments of the Church excite him, others he considers as not being applicable to him or to his circumstance, and still others appear to him as apathetical sayings of the church.

The most exciting statements are: Love God, Love your neighbor, Do good works, and Do not kill.

"The church teaches us to love God above all else," explained Chucho. "And we also must love one another. When a person loves his neighbor, he is loving God, because God is love. The law of God is difficult to fulfill, almost no one obeys it, but loving is a part of being a Catholic.

"The worst thing that you can do is harm someone," he amplified. "Let's say that you are poor. From your father you have inherited only a small house and you live by your work. Your children become sick. You come to me and ask for a loan of 500 pesos and put your house up for security. But your situation gets worse. When the time is up on the loan, I take your house. That's robbery. I am doing evil. If I am following my religion, I should say to you, 'Don't worry. Pay me when you can.' If I am rich, if I am a *rico*, I should say 'Don't worry. You don't owe me a thing.' But of course *los ricos* do not behave in that way."

"Yes," Seneca said. "Harming another person is bad. Killing a person without justification is a mortal sin. With such a sin, one cannot achieve salvation. The bandits in the mountains, because of their murders, are outside the church and cannot receive a pardon from God. When a bandit dies, he can't be buried in the cemetery. You saw those graves out by the old slaughter house. Those are the graves of bandits. The only thing their relatives can do is to pray and pray that God will forgive them. I suppose that they might obtain pardon. Christ asked forgiveness for his own murderers. But frankly, I don't think the bandits will be forgiven.

"Of course nowadays," he continued, "no one is afraid of killing another person. No one knows that it is a sin. I could not kill anybody because I am afraid of the sin and do not have the courage to kill. The reason I am afraid of the sin is not that I'm afraid of going to hell. Hell to me is a doubtful idea. I grew up with the ideas of heaven and hell, but these are ideas that no one really understands. No, the reason I do not have the courage to kill is that the sin would spot my blood and my honor. I would turn into a nothing. Also if I killed a person, I would myself be killed for 'By the rule you measure, you also shall be measured' and 'Those who kill with a knife, shall die by the knife.' "

Beyond the instructions to love and not to kill, the creeds receive summary treatment from Chucho and Seneca. The Tenth Commandment not to covet the goods of one's neighbor provoked a laugh from Seneca. "If a man is rich, you should not desire his money is what this commandment means. But no man fulfills all the commandments. A really good person may comply with two or three. A rule of the church is not to eat meat on special days. However, a poor person like me, a poor family like mine, has to eat what he has. If he has meat, he has to eat it instead of buying eggs or fish. He is not sinning; the rich person is. When the rich person has money to buy fish, and he eats meat, then he is sinning."

The *sanpedranos* do not interpret the creeds of Christianity as validating and sanctioning social action. The beatitude, "Blessed are those that hunger and thirst for justice, because they will be fulfilled," is not a call for social justice. Jorge Gaitán will not be blessed because he had a hunger for justice, but he will be blessed when his sins are forgiven. To the townsmen, Christianity has a humanizing influence on people. It makes individual people into better humans; it is not a doctrine for social revolution.

Rituals

Sunday begins early in San Pedro. At 6 A.M. religious music, interspersed with exhortations from Father Restrepo, flows out of the steeple's loudspeaker. Shortly before 8 A.M., as the priest announces who has contributed money for the forthcoming fiesta of the Virgin of Carmen, people begin to move toward the church. When the bells signal that mass is beginning, they hurry inside. A few stop to buy the two Catholic news sheets, *The Catholic Voice* and *The Peasant*, from the boy on the front steps. The money that he collects along with the amounts that he gathered from selling pictures of the Virgin and the saints will sponsor a church dance at the parish hall. Inside the church the most devout, women, children, and a few men, have already claimed their seats near the altar. In the back, near the doorway—as if they were trying to stay as far away as possible from the altar and the priest—men occupy the few remaining benches or stand near the entrance.

The women wear their best clothes and each has a delicate lace mantilla over her head. The men dress more casually in sport shirts and slacks. Several of them are barefooted. School children line the sides. The girls, all very neatly dressed in white, form on one side; the boys, the majority in black pants and white shirts, but a few in ordinary clothes and without shoes, form on the other.

Reflecting poverty, perhaps more than taste, the interior of the church is relatively simple. The churches in the Valle usually are full of statuary, the forms of which are either bland presentations of the Virgin or grotesque contortions of Jesus dangling in agony from the cross. The San Pedro statuary is mainly limited to a collection of statues surrounding the altar. The Virgin and Child stand on the right side of the altar; Saint Peter is on the left. Above the altar and dominating the church is the life-size figure of Christ nailed to the cross. Along the sides of the church are small pictures in relief that depict the incidents that occurred during Jesus' journey to his death.

The priest does not rely solely on the ritual movements to communicate to his parishioners, but he tries to educate them in the meaning of the mass. An assistant stands on a platform along one side of the church and explains to the people what the priest is doing as he progresses through the movements of the mass. A woman, Doña Jael, located out of sight in the rear of the church, sings at the appropriate intervals. For special masses she accompanies herself on the organ—for which she receives a higher wage.

The priest takes to the microphone to make a series of announcements about the forthcoming fiestas and urges the men and the boys to come work on the drainage ditch around the cemetery. Later he returns to the microphone to deliver his sermon. He calls on the people to support the president-elect, even if they are Liberals, and rails against *violencia* as action contrary to humanity, the state, and the Church. He condemns the abuse of happiness:

"Yesterday, in the small community of Bethlehem, just outside of town, the people had a fiesta for their recently married son and daughter. The fiesta, because it was a happy moment for all, continued into the night. Then the men became ignorant and like beasts. They continued drinking and drinking until like savage Indians, they began fighting each other. One man was killed and another was wounded. Why? Because the people had failed to act formally and in a manner of civilized beings. They had abused the happiness of the fiesta."

He urges people to become married. "Marriage is a holy sacrament. It is like mass; it is of Christ. People show their devotion to Christ and to the Church when they marry." He announces that the church has received food packages from the United States. "Only the poor, the very poor should ask for these packages. There are poor people in San Pedro, but there are the poor poor. For example, a mother with eight children and no husband. Only people in this state should receive these gifts." Finally, the priest calls attention to the dance to be held in the parish hall. "This dance ought to be attended. The dance is organized, well organized. The money will go to repair, once and for all, the roof of the church."

With his sermon completed, the priest turns toward the altar to prepare himself and his people for communion. A small interruption occurs when the incense burner goes out. The priest waits patiently while the altar boy struggles to light it. With the burner working once more, the mass continues. The priest lifts the chalice containing the representation of Christ's blood high and toward the statue of the crucified figure. The women up front kneel quickly, but the less devout are slow getting to their knees, and the men in the back casually drop to one knee. The school girls follow the pattern of their devout mother, while the boys resemble their father, even to the extent of spreading out a handkerchief to avoid the dust of the church floor.

After drinking from the chalice, the priest prepares the representation of Christ's body. A few women move out from the benches and toward the altar, their hands clasped together in front and their head bowed. A single man, well dressed in a suit, and a teenage boy, wrestling with his soul, are the only men to receive the sacrament. Before the communion is completed, most of the men in the back are standing up. At the sound of the final bell, the women stir themselves and gradually move toward the entrance. By the time they reach the door, the men have dispersed into the plaza. Some have already joined their less conscientious compatriots in *El Bar Central* and in *El Café*.

Ten minutes after the mass has finished, the loudspeaker in the church steeple pours out secular *corridos, cumbias,* and *bambucos.* Don Guido periodically interrupts the music with announcements about the church dance and the movie which will follow it. The movie features Miguel Mejía (a sort of Mexican Roy Rogers) who, according to Don Guido, will be "riding, fighting, and singing like never before."

The mass is an integral part of all important religious fiestas. These fiestas, which break into the normal weekly cycle of five and one half days of work and one and one half days of recreation, call for greater observance than those associated with the secular, national calendar. On a religious fiesta day, work ceases, schools and offices close, people find time to chat in the park, a few *sanpedranos* visit relatives in other towns, and with the exception of Easter Week, the men inhabit the bars.

The townspeople repeat the old Spanish saying that there are three Thursdays that cause admiration, Easter Thursday, Corpus Christi, and Ascension Thursday. July 16, the day of the Virgin Carmen, is also an important fiesta, as is November 1 when all the saints gather together. But standing out in the ritual cycle are the two seasons of Christmas and Easter.

The Christmas season begins with the fiesta of the Immaculate Conception. The fiesta testifies that while other people are infused with grace during baptism, Mary, the Mother of God, became filled with grace at the time of her conception in the womb of her mother. On the night of December 8, *sanpedranos* place candles in the windows or on the streets immediately in front of their houses. On the doorways they tack small flags of white and blue, the colors of the Virgin. The townspeople, however, are less vigorous in their display of the symbols of the Virgin's conception than are the people in the cities. In Buga, houses in the poorer sections are covered with banners, and in Cali, the well-to-do line their windows with twenty to thirty candles.

"You want to know what is the fiesta of the Immaculate Conception? pondered Doña Leonor. "Well, it is the day the Virgin died."

"What?"

"Yes, the Virgin died during the night of December 8. The candles signify that she is dead."

The fiesta of the Immaculate Conception initiates the Christmas season, but it is not until December 15 that the seasonal activities disturb the ordinary routine. In the nine days between December 15 and 24, there are, or there are supposed to be, nightly celebrations by different groups within the *municipio* of San Pedro. These groups are composed of people from a single *corregimiento* or from a single sex or age category. The priest appoints captains for each group, and the captain collects money for a mass, fireworks, and a band. On their night during the nine days, the group gathers in the park for their celebration.

As recent as eight years ago the celebrations were elaborate and well attended. Today, the captains have trouble collecting sufficient money for a celebration, and some groups completely miss their turn. The celebration of young, unmarried ladies, as one would expect, still shows considerable vigor.

The *señoritas*, following their mass, gather in front of the church. On the church steps are the members of the *municipio* band that the *señoritas* have hired. The band launches into a number, and a man lights the first fireworks of the night. These are large rockets which zoom up just above the houses and explode with a really satisfying noise. It is part of their prerogative, that on this special night, the *señoritas* can hunt for *aguinaldos*. The *señorita* approaches a person, a boy usually, and shouts out a formula, such as *pajita emboca*, (straw-in-mouth). The person sticks out his tongue and on it is a straw. If he does not have a straw, he has to give the girl a present.

The band plays, the rockets explode, and the *señoritas* chase people around the park. Someone sets fire to a cloth ball saturated with kerosene. Small boys swarm around him and start kicking the burning ball across the plaza. Many of the boys are barefooted, but they kick away with enthusiasm. If the ball rolls among the members of the band, so much the better. One man, crossing the plaza on his way home, has to hurry to get out of the way of the ball and its tail of small boys. He grumbles as he reaches the safety of his house, "Someone is going to get hurt with that ball." In *El Bar Central* men continue their nightly game of billiards and occasionally look up from their beer to see what is happening. Women, sitting in front of their houses as they have done on every other night, try to keep up their conversation about what has occurred during the day. The ball disintegrates into bits of cloth, the band breaks up, and by nine o'clock, the *señoritas* leave the park for their homes.

As Christmas Eve nears, the *sanpedranos* begin decorating their homes. No one these days builds a manger scene, a *pesebre*, but buys cardboard models from Ley or Tia, the "five and dime" stores in Tuluá. In the homes the manger scenes are erected on a table in the room fronting the street. Storekeepers and bar owners put small models on their counters. Jaime, who runs *El Café*, looked down rather proudly at his scene and explained that it represents Bethlehem, the Egyptian town where Christ was born. A few people have a Christmas tree, a small deciduous bush stripped of all its leaves and bark. They decorate the tree with imitation snow bought at the Ley.

Santa Claus or *Papá Noel* is not usually part of the decoration. Father Restrepo, in a more cosmopolitan moment, placed a large, cardboard Santa Claus in his sleigh in a corner of the Church. However, a larger manger scene with statues occupies the honored position in front of the altar.

Santa Claus is an insignificant figure because it is *El Niño de Dios*, the Christ Child, that brings the presents on the night of December 24. Seneca explained, "I was about twelve or thirteen, and I was beginning to have my doubts about the Christ Child. One Christmas Eve, I was asleep when I heard a noise in the next room. I got up to see if it was the Christ Child. When I opened the door, my father whirled around from the manger scene and would not let me look at it. He said, 'If you don't go back to bed, you'll see the Child and he won't give you a present.' I went back to bed, but I heard someone leave. I looked out the window and saw my aunt. Next morning I found a present on the manger that I knew my aunt had put there. So from then on I knew the truth about the Christ Child."

Once the parents have put the presents for their children around the manger, they go out to hear the midnight mass, the mass of the rooster. Adults exchange Christmas cards—five for a peso at Ley's—and like to send telegrams of greetings. Mothers, in particular, receive gifts from their children. Her eldest son gave Doña Leonor a radio, and she was very pleased. The rules of polite behavior required her to accept the gift with only a perfunctory word of thanks and to put it away to be quietly admired later. Doña was so thrilled with the radio that she could not contain her enthusiasm and loudly commented on its value in the presence of her son. He did not seem to mind her lack of etiquette.

December 25 is a family day. It is the one day in the year when distant sons and daughters try to return home. It is also a day of much drinking, eating, visiting, and dancing. The 28th, *El Día de los Inocentes*, is the day that King Herod had many children killed in the vain hope of destroying the Christ Child. Despite the morbid nature of the occasion, *sanpedranos*, as do all people in Spanish America and in Spain, celebrate the day by playing tricks on each other—a sort of April Fools' Day.

The end of December is another time for families to get together and to exchange visits and drinks with neighbors. After attending the midnight mass, the people go to the cemetery to hear prayers for the dead. The day is both one of happiness and sadness; there is joy for the coming year and grief for the dead relatives. The sadness disappears as the celebrations continue through January 1.

January 6 terminates the Christmas festival cycle. The 6th is *El Día de los Reyes*, the day when the three Kings came to pay homage to the Christ Child. In Spain it is the day the children receive gifts, in the colonial-like city of Popayán, it is the occasion when the rich dress in beggar clothes, in Cali, it is celebrated with a procession of big-headed buffoons, but in San Pedro, the day passes almost without notice. Only the display of the monstrance at the end of mass marks its significance.

"Christ Taught Us How To Die"

The happy rituals of Christmas, centered on life's beginning, are oriented around the holy conception of Mary and the mystical birth of Jesus. The solemn rites of Easter, centered on life's ending, revolve around the death of Christ. Of the two, it is the Easter cycle that brings the *sanpedranos* out of their homes and into the processions and into the church. However, it is not the triumph of the resurrection on Easter Sunday that calls them out, but rather the day that pulls them from their ordinary routine is Holy Friday, the day Christ died. The image around which the townspeople gather is not a radiant Christ, conquering death, but rather a thorn-crowned Jesus, suffering on the cross. The model of Christianity that they carry in their minds is not a way to redemption, but it is a blueprint on how to suffer. Chucho summed it up when he said, "Christ, in his life, taught us how to die."

The Easter season begins on Ash Wednesday, the first day of Lent. Ash Wednesday is not a sharp boundary between a preceding carnival period and a subsequent time of austerity, for the days immediately before and after it are undistinguished work days. Ash Wednesday itself only calls for a momentary journey to the church to receive a cross of ashes marked on the forehead. With the cross on his head the person returns to school or to work. He should not eat meat during the day. Since the local stores rarely have fresh fish and unless his wife makes a trip to Tuluá, he may content his conscience with a can of sardines. Only a few religiously intent people can enjoy the luxury of some personal self-denial that the Lenten days ritually call for.

The week before Easter the priest tries to prepare his parishioners for the holy days. Each evening he lectures to a few devout women on the meaning of Easter. On Holy Monday, Tuesday, and Wednesday of the Easter week, he has a series of lectures for the even smaller numbers of men.

Easter week is an intertwining of processions, services, and work-recreational patterns. The week begins on Palm Sunday with an elaborate, well-attended procession, The Procession of the Triumphant Lord. Monday, Tuesday, and Wednesday are ordinary work days, but small processions, the Good Shepherd (Monday), the Good Samaritan (Tuesday), and Jesus in the Garden (Wednesday) pass quickly through the streets during the evening hours. Thursday, Friday, and Saturday are days when work stops, and drinking and music are prohibited. Thursday commemorates the founding of the Church and the Priesthood. Friday, the day of Christ's death, equals Thursday in ritual importance, and its procession, The Stations of the Cross, matches the one of Palm Sunday in quality and attendance. Saturday and its Procession of Loneliness pass quickly and quietly. A special mass at Saturday midnight terminates the three day period of silence. Activities on Sunday, the day of Christ's resurrection, are limited to a small procession; otherwise it resembles an ordinary Sunday, complete with music, drinking, and visiting. Palm Sunday, Holy Thursday, and Holy Friday stand out as the most meaningful days in the Easter cycle.

Palm Sunday reenacts Jesus' triumphant march into Jerusalem. At 8 in the morning people begin congregating at the steps of the church. The crowd is extremely large for a *sanpedrano* religious affair and numbers at least 100. Most are children and most of the children are girls. Perhaps as many as five adult men stand at the fringe of the crowd. The children carry branches of palm leaves which range in size from a twig to giant branches 15 feet in height. Don Guido, standing on the steps and gossiping with a small group of mothers, explains with a giggle that once the palms are blessed they are good for warding off lightning.

Doña Jaél, the choirmistress, is arguing with Father Restrepo over a point in the organization of the procession and stabs an authoritative finger at a book that she is holding. The Father suddenly turns to a group of teenage boys passing by and calls out for them to come and carry the statues. They grin sheepishly at each other and eventually position themselves at the handles of the platforms upon which the statues stand. They lift up the figures and the procession gets under way.

The procession is going to the back of town to meet the figure of King Christ. Then with Christ the King seated on a burro, the procession will move back through town and end at the church. At the head of the procession are three boys dressed in bright robes and carrying silver poles on top of which are candles and a cross. Following them is a small figure, an angel according to Doña Leonor, but who resembles a young girl dressed in a white pinafore. The figure stands on a platform which has two handles on either end. The handles rest on the shoulders of two boys. Father Restrepo follows, then comes the twelve "disciples," twelve small boys dressed in bright red, purple, green, and pink robes. Doña Jaél hovers about them and gets them to stay reasonably close together. Behind the disciples are two more statues, "John the Baptist" and Mary Magdalene. Their vacant porcelain eyes contrast with their warm-colored clothes which sway to the tilt of the carriers' uneven gait. The teenage boys are replaced with men, and these periodically shout to their friends standing in the doorways to come and take their turn at carrying John and Mary Magdalene. Children file along either side of the disciples and the statues and wave their palm branches. Some of the boys make whistles from the leaves, and the whistles' shrills adds to the general noise of chatter, calls, and greetings.

The procession comes to the meeting spot in the back of town. Two men and a woman are trying to place a figure of King Christ on a burro. The statue is wooden and has moveable arms and legs. One of the men is the eldest Lozano brother. He says to Father Restrepo, "Just a minute, Father. We will have him ready shortly."

"Hand me the hammer," he asks his assistant. "I'll nail his leg to this part of the pack saddle. Watch it! Hold the burro."

"That ought to do it," he concludes and steps aside to allow the woman to arrange the clothes over the wooden figure. "OK, Father. We're ready."

Lozano steps in front of the burro and grasps the lead rope while Father Restrepo sprinkles holy water on the figure and blesses it. "Let me get in front of you," Lozano shouts to the men carrying the statues. He moves into a position in between the statues and the apostles.

Doña Jaél had stopped the apostles about a block away because she did not want them to walk through the mud that covered the back streets. So the procession is strung out, the priest and the three boys are in front, the angel next, then the disciples, then a large gap filled with children and palm branches. Behind them trudges the burro with Christ swagging precariously on his back. The statues of John and Mary Magdalene closely follow. People come to their doorways to watch the procession pass by. The men take off their hats, and a few people cross themselves as the figure of Christ passes by. Some of the participants drop out; others wave to their friends and relatives.

Despite Lozano's weight on the lead rope, the burro moves very slowly. One of the men moves behind the burro and tries to push. "He needs gasoline," Lozano grins. A boy rushes up, "Father Restrepo says hurry. He is almost to the highway." Then the burro stops. Lozano pulls; the other man pushes, but the best they can do is to get the burro to lift a foot which he puts back in the same spot. "He needs more than gasoline," Lozano stops in exasperation. "Go get your burro. Maybe he will move. No, wait. Here comes Doña Maria." A woman, the owner of the burro, steps out of the small crowd, grabs the lead rope and pulls. The burro takes a few reluctant steps and then begins to move steadily ahead.

The procession moves to the highway and goes down one side. Buses pull over to the side, and the passengers crowd to the windows to watch. Suddenly there it is. A clean, coherent image of the burro, the figure of Christ, and Doña Maria emerges out of the backdrop of buses and people. Doña Maria, her dark brown face as expressless as her stolid body, leans patiently against the lead rope. The burro's walk, formerly a stumbling, comical gait, changes to a calm, majestic stride. The thin, artificial figure of Christ and his doll-like face are cold contrasts to the warm, comforting animalism of the burro and of the woman. And the mind stretches out to recall countless small town processions patiently carrying their religion through the streets of the world. Then the image dissolves into reality, its magic disappears, and the moment that all anthropologists are driven to search for is gone. It will not be back.

The procession turns from the highway and cuts across the plaza to the church. Men remove the Christ figure from the burro, and as they carry it up the steps, Father Restrepo shouts out,

"Viva Christ the King!"
   "Viva!" the crowd responds.
"Viva the Catholic Faith."
   "Viva!"
"Viva the Sacred Heart of Jesus."
   "Viva!"
"Viva the studious youths."
   "Viva!"

People then enter the church for mass and the blessing of the palms.

Monday, Tuesday, and Wednesday, like their small, evening processions, slip quietly by. An early short, "spoken" mass begins Holy Thursday, but the major ritual is at four in the afternoon. This is the mass that commemorates the first communion and the establishment of the Church and Priesthood.

Just before he begins the mass, Father Restrepo hurries from his activities in the front of the church to the side where the confession booth is located. The booth has three parts: the center portion, where the priest sits, and the two side sections, where the confessors kneel. The priest's section is separated from the other portions by walls in which are small, shuttered windows. The priest sits facing outward, and he can communicate through the windows only by awkwardly turning the top portion of his body. His section has no door to shut out the noise of the congregation. The confessors' sections have half doors which only partially shield them from noise and view.

When the priest sits down, lines of people, mostly women, quickly form on either side of the booth. A woman on the right side enters the booth, the priest swivels his head and opens the window to hear her confession. In three minutes, she has finished and leaves. The priest swivels to the other side to hear the next person. In five minutes this confession is completed. The priest turns back to his right for the next woman. In the space of thirty minutes, he hears ten confessions.

While Father Restrepo is hearing the confessors, some of whom are confessing for the first time since last Easter, the church continues to fill. People shuffle about and whisper to each other; some go down to the altar rail to pray, but others stand impatiently in the back. The priest terminates the confessions and hurries back to the front. The rackets, which replace the bells for the three day period of silence, begin clacking, there is a shuffle in the back as the last minute arrivals crowd in, and the mass begins.

The ceremony of the mass differs from other ones only in the replacement of the bells with the wooden rackets and in the singing of the Gloria. The husky, plaintive voice of Doña Jaél is joined with those of four other women. Their mingled voices gently fill the church and are softly beautiful. More people go to the altar rail to take communion, but otherwise the congregation behaves in much the same fashion as it does in regular services. The devout women in front of the church kneel at each correct interval; behind them, the less devout kneel only now and again; and in the back, the men go down on one knee when the priest holds up the host.

After communion, the priest places the host in the monstrance and removes the monstrance from its place above the altar. A procession is formed similar to the other times when the monstrance is displayed, except the *personero* replaces the *alcalde* who is unable to attend. The procession moves slowly around the church and then stops at an alcove. The priest places the monstrance in the alcove and there it will stay for the night. People in family groups will come during the night to pray before the monstrance and to ask for assistance. Father Restrepo turns from the alcove and begins talking to the congregation, but the people ignore him and begin to leave. Except for the people coming out of the church, the plaza is nearly empty. Over in *El Bar Central*, however, the desolatory clink of wooden balls comes out the doorway.

On Holy Friday ritual activity reaches a peak. In the morning the Procession of the Stations of the Cross moves through the streets. In the afternoon, at three, the hour of Jesus' death, the priest delivers the traditional Sermon of Seven Words. He takes the words that Jesus uttered while on the cross and elaborates each into a discourse. The sermon, amplified by the loudspeaker system, reverberates through the town for two hours. At eight in the evening the priest again delivers an oration; this time he evokes the image of Jesus being taken from the cross and placed in the tomb. Following the oration, the *municipio* officials join with the priest to act out the event. They take the figure of Christ down from its position over the altar and place it in an alcove which functions as a symbolic tomb. There the figure remains until the midnight mass on Saturday when, in commemoration of the resurrection, it is restored to its place above the altar.

The most visible rite of the day, the one whose evocative images occupy a larger portion of the town's space and call out a greater number of its people, is the procession, The Stations of the Cross. The procession retraces Jesus' journey up the Hill of Calvary. At dawn *municipio* workers cut small trees from the banks of San Pedro Creek and implant them along the route. The trees stand for those that grew on Calvary. As the work progresses people come out of their homes to help. Two houses have no trees in front of them and their doors are tightly closed. These are the homes of the Protestants.

The line of trees goes from the plaza to the highway and then turns back into town; after curling around several blocks, it ends at the street nearest the church entrance. At several corners are established the "stations." Here awaiting the procession are small clusters of people grouped around an item, usually a statue, that will be added to the march.

When the procession starts at the church, it consists only of a statue of Jesus. Four men carry the platform upon which the statue stands to the first station. They lower the platform and place a large cross across the statue's shoulders. Just behind the figure of Jesus they put a statue dressed in the uniform of a Roman soldier. The soldier has a short whip in his hand. When they raise the platform to their shoulders, the scene is Jesus, his head crowned with thorns and his body bent under the weight of the cross, and the soldier, his face strangely contorted as in pain and his arm raised to lash the struggling figure in front of him. Doña Jaél, giving voice to an ancient attitude, later remarked, "The soldier was a Jew."

While the procession is on its way to the next station, the women sing in a mournful key. Most of them are dressed in black, although here and there is a young girl in white. The men walk in the back. There are more men than in any other procession, and for a number of the older men, this is their first procession for the Easter week. A little over half of the men are wearing suits, and a few, the poorest of all, are barefooted. The procession reaches the next station. The priest starts a prayer; the people stop singing and gradually kneel, the men protecting their clothes with handkerchiefs. When the priest finishes the people rise, and four men pick up the platform which supports Mary, the Mother of Jesus. She is dressed as the Queen of Heaven and wears a black robe sprinkled with stars. On her head is a crown. The procession starts forward, the thorn-crowned figure of the suffering Jesus leading the way. Mary is moved to a position behind him, and the women sing their lament once again.

As the procession passes the stations, additional figures, Mary Magdalene; John, the Beloved Disciple; and Peter, the First Pope, move into the line. At one station two statues of women dressed in black await the procession. The smaller figure holds between her hand a handkerchief on which is imprinted the agonizing face of Christ. She is one of the three Marys whom Jesus encountered on his way to Calvary. She had given him a handkerchief to wipe the sweat from his face, and when he returned it, the outline of his face was fixed on the cloth.

The procession, once all the figures from the various stations have been added to it, turns toward the church. It seems to move on two levels, the lower, human one and the upper, statue one. Paradoxically, the statues, the artificial portraits of the supreme mythical figures, assume an individuality greater than that of the mass of people below them. They appear to take on life, and led by the figure bent under a cross, they go striding down the street on the backs of their worshippers.

The rituals of Holy Week are the rituals of Holy Thursday and Friday— the days that Christ established his church through the commemorative sacrifice of communion; the days that he suffered and died. All other rituals lead up to or depart from these two days. The gay march of Palm Sunday elevates the popular victory of Jesus so that his denunciation, his alienation, and his death will strike deeper into the senses. On the other side of the two holy days, the rituals of Saturday and Sunday dissolve Holy Week into the ordinary cycle of activities. In

San Pedro Resurrection Sunday, the day which North Americans, particularly Protestants, greet the morning sun with shouts of "Halleluya, Christ has arisen," is a return to a normal day.

Across the Colombian countryside, among the peasants of Cundinamarca, the people of Saucío do not "fully conceive of the redemptive role of Christ," but rather they depict Christ as "the long-suffering, thorn-crowned Son of God, nailed to a cross and resigned to His death . . ." (Fals-Borda 1955:228). In the city of Buga, in the famous basilica of Our Lord of Miracles, the walls rebound with figures in agony. Along one wall a beautifully carved coffin rests on a low stand. The side of the coffin facing the church is made of glass, and through the glass one can see a full-length figure of a dead Christ. He is naked except for a small breech cloth. His skin has a pale, greyish color. The wounds on his hands and his feet are a dull red. The skin around the wounds are puckered, realistically copying the condition caused by the removal of the nails. An immaculately dressed woman enters the church and kneels at the coffin; her handsome face lowers to the level of the dead figure. She prays silently.

"No, this is not fatalism," insisted Chucho. "It is realism. Christ died so that we too could learn how to suffer and how to die. To live is to die. It is part of the human tragedy. Through his actions, Christ teaches us this tragedy and how we must face death."

"When Jesus was on his way to the cross, would not it have been better if he had fought against his persecutors?"

"No. He wanted to set an example. He wanted to show us how to suffer patiently, how to accept death with tranquility. Today, humans do not suffer correctly nor formally. They do not patiently await the outcome. They fight against death. This is because they do not have the image of Christ in their minds. Because we are humans, we cannot die in the manner of Christ, who was God. But we must try. If God suffered patiently, then surely we must do likewise. We must try to conform to death. This is the reason why Holy Friday is more important than Resurrection Sunday."

6

The Family Side

Seneca and His Kin

SENECA, HIS MOTHER, and his siblings live in a house located between the plaza and the back part of town. Back of Seneca's place the houses are often made of wattle and daub and have thatched roofs and dirt floors, while toward the plaza and the highway, the houses are frequently constructed of kiln-dried brick and have a concrete facade. Seneca's house is adobe brick with a tile roof and floor but has no facade. In preparation for his coming marriage Seneca is having his house remodeled. In contrast to Doña Jaél's husband, who secured a loan from the *Caja Agraria*, Seneca is using the money he won from the lottery. He is paying one of his younger brothers, Jaime, to extend the roof over the patio to make a new room and to re-plaster and to white-wash the whole structure.

The small room that faces the street is the sleeping quarters of Seneca and his brother, Hemberson. Through this room the door opens onto the patio. In a sheltered portion of the patio is the dining table and a few straight back chairs. Above the table is a picture of Jesus in the Garden, a shelf supporting a small radio, and photographs of several soccer teams. Seneca is a serious soccer fan and plays on the occasional teams that sporadically form in San Pedro. He spends his Sunday afternoons glued to the radio listening to the fortunes of the Cali team. Every two months or so, he goes to Cali to see the team play. He enters the stadium at the earliest possible moment and spends the long waiting period trying to dispell the increasing nervous tension. As the team comes out on the field, he becomes quiet and still, "full of fear."

"I was born here in San Pedro and went to school here. I got to the fourth grade without repeating, but in the fourth, the big boys distracted me and I learned nothing. So I had to repeat it.

"After I finished primary school, I went to an agricultural school in Andalucia, a town north of here. I studied there for two and a half years, but my family did not have enough money for me to continue. I came back home and

79

A fiesta in the patio of Seneca's father-in-law. (Photograph by Thomas Schorr.)

worked in the fields. I worked for a while in my uncle Chucho's factory and for a few weeks in Don Mario's, who is my uncle by marriage.

"I wasn't earning much, about 40 cents a day, so I left Don Mario and worked for a year in the Tobacco Institute in Tuluá. I heard about the job of Forest Inspector from one of my friends. He was the Inspector at that time, but he was going to become *municipio* treasurer. He told me that employees of the *municipio* usually got first chance at any vacant position, so I got a job as *municipio* night watchman. Because I was a good watchman and because of my training at the agricultural school, I was made Forest Inspector of the *Municipio* of San Pedro. Anyone that wants to cut down a tree has to get my permission."

Like many people in San Pedro, Seneca is at the fringes of Colombia's economic system. His constant shifting from one job to another reflects both the ephemeral nature of the jobs that he can hold and his restless search for a better position, one with more money and more *cultura*. He is continually scanning the universe of San Pedro and constantly compiling data on where he stands in the scheme of opportunities. He compulsively gathers information on the values of articles; the price of a watch, a fountain pen, a bicycle, or of a kerosene stove goes into his mind to be quickly assessed as to where the owner stands relative to Seneca.

The scale of valuable things runs from faith to food. Although faith is unique in that its value cannot be depleted, it is a scarce commodity and is "worth more" than the mass. When Seneca is with the *alcalde* on a tour of the outlying *corregimientos*, people occasionally give them small gifts of food, an avocado, a pineapple, or a coconut. Seneca eagerly accepts the gifts for they are items having value which he is getting free. He curls his body around the food and consumes it with vigorous greed.

Because most items in Seneca's world are like food—very scarce and have high value—he travels through his universe alert for those who would take things from him. Thieves, and more importantly, the fear of thieves, terrorize him in much the same fashion that witches haunted his colonial ancestors. During the day the door of his house is not opened to just any *sanpedrano*, for that person may be a thief on reconnaissance. Each night he and his family seal themselves in their rooms, and any noise they hear is likely to be that of a thief trying to enter.

The most important person to Seneca, more important than his bride, is his mother.

"I like to collect thoughts. I write them down in a composition book. One night I was sitting in *El Bar Central* with some friends of mine. We decided to see who had the best thoughts. Everyone said theirs, and then it became my turn. I had time to think, and I remembered a poem I wrote about mothers. I said the poem and all agreed that it was the most beautiful. Don Guido recited it over the loudspeaker on the night of December 31.

"The worst thing you can call someone, the ugliest words you can say, is 'son of a whore.'

"I'm the eldest son in my family, and I have to look after my mother. Because my father is dead, I have a heavy responsibility. Last night I didn't get much sleep. My mother is sick, and I had to get up to see to her and to give her the medicine that the doctor told me to buy."

Doña Lola is a quiet, unassuming person. The death of her husband has made her unexpectedly poor, but she carries herself with a dignity that comes from being a member of a good family. She devotes all of her time to the care of her family. With Seneca's help, each Sunday morning she gives her house a thorough cleaning. The presence of electricity and piped water has made her tasks easier. Yet the water system frequently fails, and at times, like during Holy Week, it becomes heavy with mud. When this occurs, she sends Guillermo, her youngest, to the San Pedro Creek for water.

She prepares the family meals in a wattle and daub kitchen built on the back of the house. Until Seneca brought a two-burner kerosene stove on credit, she used an open hearth built against one wall of the kitchen. Periodically, a woodcutter came by to sell her small quantities of dry wood. Now, she sends Guillermo for kerosene from the store down the street. The evening meal is the largest one she prepares. She sets the table with rice, manioc, potatoes, a bit of chopped lettuce with a slice of tomato, and a chunk of beef. For special days she kills a hen from the small flock she keeps in the *solar*. At times there is milk on the table, but always there is hot chocolate or *agua de panela*—brown sugar melted in warm water.

While her family is eating at the table, Doña Lola stays in the kitchen, eating bits from the pots as she cleans them. After the meal is over and the cleaning finished, she takes a chair from the patio, opens the street door, and sits down to enjoy the evening and conversation with her neighbors. She rarely goes to stroll in the park.

Raquel is the next in age to Seneca. She is the town *telefonista* and operates the single phone that connects San Pedro to the other cities in the Valle. She always appears well groomed and is mildly conscious of the distinction between herself and a sharecropper's daughter.

Two of Seneca's sisters, one of which is older than he, have married and have left San Pedro. One lives in Bogotá; the other is in Cali. Seneca scarcely mentions them, and they rarely return to San Pedro. Hemberson, the next brother, is in the process of leaving. Since Seneca has taken on the responsibilities of an eldest son, Hemberson is freed to discover other opportunities. He is not hostile to Seneca but is apathetical to him. They move about in the same town and in the same house but rarely touch each other.

Hemberson has not yet decided to make the break from his family and presently contents himself at working in whatever happens to be locally available. He worked for a while for his uncle, Chucho, taking care of the chicken house. Then he and Climaco, Chucho's partner, came to a sharecropping agreement, and Hemberson is trying, not too successfully, to raise tomatoes on a *plaza* of Climaco's land.

"I can't help you today. I have to go see about Jaime. Yesterday, he 'robbed' his sweetheart, or better said, they went off together without her parents' permission. Last night her parents denounced Jaime to the judge, and the judge put him in jail for eight days.

"Yes, this happens from time to time. When one of the parents, for example the mother, doesn't like the boy, he 'robs' the girl, if she is willing. Later on they get married. But Jaime says he isn't going to marry the girl. If he would, they would let him out of jail. But he says he doesn't want to. Why? Well, Jaime says that the girl, well, that the girl isn't, you know, isn't a *señorita.*"

Before the week was up, Jaime's resolve could not outlast the squalor of the San Pedro jail, so he agreed to marry. He moved his few possessions from his mother's house over to his bride's parents'.

Seneca's youngest sister, Felícita, is a good daughter. She worked hard helping her mother. She rarely left the house and did not have a boyfriend. Then she decided to enter a convent in Bogotá. "I don't really know why. She has always enjoyed going to church and has talked about becoming a nun. She just likes that sort of thing."

Seneca decided to take his sister to Bogotá in Velotax, a long distance taxi service, and went to Cali to buy the tickets. When he returned to San Pedro, he discovered that the agent had sold him out of date tickets. So he had to find someone to loan him the money to buy a new set of tickets.

Guillermo, the youngest, goes to San Pedro's primary school. He always is dressed neatly and wears shoes. "Being an eldest brother is hard. Today I had to get my *hermanito* out of trouble. He and one of his friends took a bicycle and went to Buga. I had to go get him and pay the owner of the bicycle."

In addition to these relatives, the people who share his living space, Seneca has a number of other kindred in *sanpedrano* households. The closest of these extended relatives are his maternal grandmother, his maternal uncle (Chucho), and two maternal aunts. One of the aunts is married to Mario Tascón, the cigar maker, and the other is married to the owner of the only private two story building in town. Seneca has no paternal relatives in San Pedro.

"Our family exists on the salaries of Raquel and of mine. Hemberson never contributes anything. My other relatives do not help. You know, it is true what they say. One receives more help from an acquaintance than from a relative.

"When my father died, I had to leave agriculture school. We didn't have any money, and my grandmother, who does, would not give me any.

"My uncle, Chucho, loves me, but he will not contribute to our household. Neither will my aunts. When my mother, their sister, was very sick, I had to go to Buga to borrow money for medicine. I borrowed it from a friend of Chucho's. Chucho loves me. He will speak for me, and he spoke to this friend, but he doesn't loan me money. When I worked for him, he paid me less than he paid a non-relative.

"Look here. See this bill. This is what I owe the store here in San Pedro for groceries and other things. I've spent my salary buying medicine for my mother. But the storekeeper wants his money. It is December and there are many expenses. We should have the house white-washed. This is the reason I play the lottery. My relatives won't help me, my salary is not large, and always someone is sick. So I have to put my luck in the lottery.

"Will you speak to the head of your *misión* about me? You know me. You can help me. You can speak for me. Speak to him, won't you."

Seneca did not ask his brothers to help him add the extra room on to his mother's house. Instead he paid Jaime a daily wage, which Seneca reckoned to include the lunch that Jaime's mother prepared him. The wage was lower than that normally paid to a day laborer.

Beyond the extended relatives Seneca has another group of people with whom he has quasi-kinship ties. These persons are the members of his *compadrazco*, his godparent system.

The *compadrazco* is composed of individuals who agree to sponsor a child or a young adult at the church rituals of baptism, confirmation, and marriage. The baptismal sponsors are far more important than the godparents of confirmation and marriage. When a couple makes ready to have their young infant baptized, they decide who will be the child's godparents. They ask one man to act as *padrino* and one woman to be the *madrina*. The *padrino* and *madrina* agree at the baptism that they will attend to their godchild's spiritual instruction and that if the parents die, they will assume the responsibility for their *ahijado*'s upbringing.

"I am going to be a *padrino* of a friend who is getting married tomorrow. All I have to do is to sponsor my friend. I don't have to help with the expenses or anything like that. My friend is only having one *padrino* and his bride only one *madrina*. But a person can have as many as he wants, three, four, five, maybe more. At confirmation, however, there is only one. If a girl is being confirmed, she has a *madrina*; if it is a boy, he has a single *padrino*.

"My baptismal *padrino* is Don Leonardo Tascón. He has a large hacienda across the highway. It runs from the highway to the river. He lives in Cali. He and my father were good friends, and they helped each other. Don Leonardo is president of the Liberal party's *departamento* directorate. His cousin was governor of the Valle several years back. My father, of course, was also a Liberal, and he would help Don Leonardo in political matters. In return, Don Leonardo assisted my father in securing positions. Father was the *alcalde* of Vijes, a town across the river, and he wanted to change. I can't remember why. Perhaps he was tired of Vijes, or maybe the people, who are mostly Conservatives, did not respect him. At any rate, he talked to Don Leonardo, and Don Leonardo got him the *alcalde* position here in San Pedro.

"Don Leonardo loved my father. He offered to send him to school in Bogotá so my father could have a title. But my father didn't want to go.

"Because of this friendship between him and Don Leonardo, my father asked him to be my *padrino*. This made them *compadres*. No, Don Leonardo did not become my father's co-parent because he wanted my father's help. Neither did my father ask Don Leonardo to be my *padrino* because Don Leonardo was rich. They were friends before I was born. Because they were friends, they became *compadres*."

"Which is more important? The relationship between co-parents, or the relationship between godparent and godson? In my opinion the relation between *padrino* and *ahijado* is more important. The *padrino* agrees at baptism to take care of his *ahijado*. He doesn't say a word about his *compadre*."

"When my father died, my *padrino* helped me a lot, or rather he helped my family. He gave us tiles to repair our house, and he gave Hemberson a job at his hacienda. He still helps us. He gave us the wood to build the new room. When I took Felícita to Bogotá, I stayed in the building that he owns there. Practically every year he gives me a present on Christmas. He even offered to send me back to school, but I'm too stupid.

"I don't like to go to him and ask a lot of favors. Hemberson, who spends more time at Don Leonardo's hacienda than I do, says I'm sentimental. I don't know, but it is crude to go to Don Leonardo every time I need something."

"Yes, Seneca is my *ahijado*. In the *municipio* of San Pedro I guess I have about two hundred *ahijados*. One day in Buenos Aires, that small community in the mountains above San Pedro, I obtained twenty-five godchildren. My relations with the people of San Pedro are good. They are sound people; they respect property rights."

Don Carlos, the tailor, has two apprentices working with him. One of them is his *ahijado*. His *ahijado*'s father and Don Carlos are good friends, and he is the *padrino* of Don Carlos' daughter. Carlos charges the other apprentice $100 for the total period of apprenticeship, but he charges his *ahijado* a small weekly sum plus each day's supply of milk.

Don Carlos observes that the obligations of the *compadrazco*, the responsibilities of godfather to godson and the mutual assistance between co-parents, are frequently *cosas simbólicas*. The system is a symbolic thing, and it depends on the *voluntad*, the will, of each partner for its success. Often the partners prefer not to will the system into action. The *municipio* judge comments that nowadays *compadres* do not respect each other. They do not give formality to their relations. Instead of addressing each other with the polite *Usted*, they use the intimate *tu*.* They treat their *compadres* like they treat any close acquaintance, with *confianza* instead of *respeto*. Father Restrepo agrees that now the system is honored in name only. Doña Leonor caustically points out that when her husband left her, no *padrinos* of her children offered assistance. Don Guido compares the times of today with those of his youth and concludes that the loss of the fear of God and creeping modernism has all but destroyed the meaning of *compadre*, *padrino*, and *ahijado*.

Types of Families

Seneca's family is in the process of remolding itself. The process began with the death of Seneca's father which transformed a male led household to a female led one. The two oldest sisters left to form their families, and Seneca, as the eldest son of a widowed mother, began to take on the responsibilities of financing the house and seeing to the affairs of its younger members. As he matures, he gathers in more of these obligations. Raquel finds a unique job for a *sanpedrana* and contributes to the family upkeep. Hemberson is on the verge of leaving the family; Jaime does leave and goes to live in his bride's house located on the outskirts of town. Felícita goes to Bogotá to become a nun, and only Guillermo remains in school.

As the members of the family mature and leave, the structure of the family changes back from a female led to a male led one, but with the eldest son replacing the dead father. When Seneca marries, the family moves rapidly into a new form. The core of the new type will be Seneca, his wife, and their children; his mother and the remaining unmarried siblings will metamorphose into attachments. Once the mother dies and the last sibling departs, a completely new nuclear family, Seneca's, will finally emerge.

If the sequence of changes that are occurring not only in Seneca's family but also in the other *sanpedrano* families is frozen, and frozen in 1962–1963, two contrasting types of families appear in the town. One type is nuclear versus extended. A nuclear family is minimally composed of a conjugal pair, married or common-law. An extended family is minimally composed of a consanguineal pair, for example, a mother and her adult son, but it is usually two conjugal pairs related to each other through kinship, for example, a man, his wife, their daughter and her husband. The second contrast type is patriarchal versus matriarchal. A family is patriarchal when the husband-father is called the head of the household; it is matriarchal when the wife-mother is designated head. The two contrast types cross cut each other; for example, a patriarchal family may be either nuclear or

---

* *Sanpedranos* use both *tu* and the older *vos* for intimate address.

extended. In addition to the two types of families there are six isolates, four women and two men, who have neither spouse nor kinsman in San Pedro. The number and percentage of each type are:

Nuclear-Extended
Nuclear	150	71%
Extended	63	29%
Total	213	100%

Patriarchal-Matriarchal
Patriarchal	163	77.5%
Matriarchal	50	22.5%
Total	213	100 %

Nuclear versus Extended

The much higher frequency of the nuclear type reflects the town concept that a new couple should set up a household independent of either set of parents. While a *sanpedrano* should respect his mother-in-law, it is best to completely avoid the problem and live separately from her. Even then, she may make a nuisance of herself.

Unlike the nuclear type, which is largely a homogeneous category, the extended type includes several variations. A family may be extended either lineally or laterally. A lineal expansion may go up to include an aged parent or down to encompass a child, its spouse, and/or children. A lateral extension may go through a brother, sister, or cousin, and include their spouses and/or children.

The lineal extension is more frequent. Forty-seven household heads have a parent or a child, usually a daughter and her children, attached to their families. Only sixteen families are extended laterally; half of these extensions are through sisters. In sum, the extended type can vary from an adult son and his mother to a man, his mother, his wife, married children, their wives, their children, and unmarried offspring.

For the most part the extended families represent one or another of the temporary stages in the constant evolution of the nuclear core. However, when a household head owns his house and has a sizeable amount of land, as in the case of the senior Lozano, the extended nature of his family has a more permanent quality about it. Yet even in this case when the senior Lozano dies, his younger sons will probably divide up their inheritance and go their separate ways. The eldest son will remain at the homeplace to manage what is left of the farm and to care for his mother.

Patriarchal versus Matriarchal

The patriarchal family, guided through life's tempests by a stern but benevolent father, is the model type. How many husband-fathers of the 163 patriarchal families actually wield the power in their families is a matter that even the husband-fathers do not know. One Sunday afternoon, Don Carlos, Pedro, and

Ramón were talking about the way they run their families. Ramón had just finished saying that the man has the right to expect his wife to obey him. Carlos added, "I know of a case where the woman is of a higher class than her husband, and because she has more money, she can dominate the man. But I agree with you. When the man and the woman are of the same class, then he dominates the woman. Like in my family."

Just then Don Carlos' wife appeared at the door. "Carlos," she said. "The goats need milking." With neither a word nor glance, Don Carlos rose and left.

Whatever may be the outcome of a young man's hopes for real power in his family, to begin that family he takes his bride to church for the marriage ceremony. There are alternate ways of setting up a new household. A young couple can make a common-law agreement, or they can have a civil ceremony. From the man's standpoint, a common-law union, a *union libre*, usually means that he is not ready to establish a patriarchal family, for most free unions result in a matriarchal family. On the other hand, the vast majority of the 163 patriarchal families, where the man is at least the nominal head, are composed of church married couples.

Few *sanpedranos* think seriously of a civil ceremony. They accept the church's position that marriage is not genuine unless it is performed before a priest. A civil ceremony carries a greater stigma than a free union. Common-law marriage is older than the civil ceremony, and it is relatively neutral. A civil ceremony is something new, somewhat like accepting Protestantism, and like Protestantism it is an act, an open act, against the Church and Colombia. So a young man ready to follow the ideals of his culture, ready to assert his formality, ready to become the head of his household, and having finished testing the morals of his sweetheart and having asked her father, meets his bride before the priest.

Seneca approached his bride's father and received only lukewarm approval. Pleased by the fact that his love refused his advances, he continued to hope that the father would agree. The wedding date was tentatively set on several occasions, and once the father flatly refused. However, when Seneca won his $1000, both he and his prospective father-in-law changed. This time when Seneca made his request, he did so with confident expectations. The father, realizing that his future son-in-law was now a man of substance and that his daughter would be well cared for, gave his consent.

The ceremony took place at six in the morning in a church in Tuluá. Only a single *padrino* and a *madrina* were selected, and only a few friends and relatives attended. The bride's father and Seneca's sister from Cali were the only close relatives present. Seneca explained that he did not have the wedding in San Pedro because too many people would be looking at him.

Once the actual ceremony was over and the party had returned to San Pedro, the urgent desire for privacy, the almost stealthy atmosphere, disappeared. The guests spent most of the day drinking and eating in the bride's parents' house. Earlier they had sent their gifts to Seneca and his bride through an intermediary, the polite, correct way. Now they were paying more attention to each other than to the newly married couple. The couple, singly or together, flittered around the edges of the fiesta, the bride helping her mother with the guests, the groom disappearing momentarily to see to the affairs of his mother's house. They demonstrated little overt affection for each other.

Fifty of the families in San Pedro are headed by women. Nearly half of these matriarchies are products of widowhood. Seven of them are headed by women who describe themselves as the heads of their household although their husbands are alive and live with them. Nearly all of the seven women own the house that they and their husbands are occupying. The remainder of the matriarchal types, twenty-one, are headed by women who, instead of marrying, have established a common-law pact with a man. In the majority of these "true" matriarchies the man has left, and the woman has to rely on her own labor to finance the household and to bring up her children.

The presence of the "true" matriarchal pattern in a highly Catholic, male dominated culture is at first difficult to comprehend. However, Doña Leonor makes the observations that *en Colombia hay mucha libertad, pero las leyes son distintas.** The legalistic formal rules of Colombian culture are systematically ignored to the degree they are severe; the more strict the law, the more liberty a person takes. The imposition of requirements from the elite begets alternatives at the local level. One alternative to marriage is free union.

The alternative of free union is an acceptable one. It is much more acceptable than a civil ceremony, and it is not in the same class as sexual promiscuity, adultery, or concubinage. The local priest voices a common view when he says that the partners in a free union are often good people, who live worthy lives. Many times, as they approach old age, they marry and give legitimacy to themselves and to their children.

From a man's point of view a free union is a product of a woman's lack of morality. When a man has a girl friend, he tries, and to be a man, he must try, to have sexual relations with her, before he will consider marriage. If she lets him, then he will not marry her. However, he may agree to a free union, to *juntarse* instead of *casarse.* So it is up to the girl. If she wants marriage, she resists his advances; if she wants to "join" with him, she accedes to his sexual demands.

"No, that is not the way it is," said Doña Leonor. "Let me explain the real nature of free union. If a woman marries a man, she has lost all of her freedom. If her husband decides to have a concubine, or worse, if he decides to leave her, she can do nothing. She has to support herself and her children the best way she can.

"She cannot do like her husband and live with another man. Why? No, it is not a sin, but her husband, when he finds out, may come back and kill her. Remember Carmen? That's what may happen."

Carmen was a pretty, vivacious young mother. Her husband had gone, and she was supporting herself as a seamstress in San Pedro. She used to visit Doña Leonor and chatted with her while Doña was preparing the anthropologist's supper. One evening, the anthropologist said good night to both women and was walking across the plaza when he heard Carmen call, "Hey *mister*, wait a minute." He stopped and Carmen came to him. "That was very interesting what you were telling Doña Leonor about the United States," she said in a warm, open voice. "Why don't

---

* "In Colombia there is much liberty, but the laws are different." This is Doña Leonor's version of the famous Spanish-American phrase "I obey, but I do not comply." While laws are very rigid, people agree to ignore them.

you come to see me, and we can talk some more." The anthropologist thought to himself, "Now wait a minute, Miles. Women don't stop men in the middle of the plaza this way. On the other hand, she may only want to be friendly, which is nice. Still. . . ." He replied in what he hoped was a non-committal manner, "OK, one day I will."

About two months later, Carmen's husband shot her as she came out of a Tuluá hotel.

"Doña, if a woman is scared of her husband and he has left her, why doesn't she divorce him?"

"No. Divorce is bad. It is a serious sin. You have many divorces in the United States, don't you. Colombia is better than the United States. Now, if a woman agrees to a free union, she is better off. If she and her husband like each other, then perhaps eventually she will agree to marry. If her common-law husband leaves her, so what? She can go to live with another man. Her first husband, because he was not married to her, has no claim on her. She can go live with another man, or she can marry. So with free union, you see, a woman has more freedom. She has more alternatives. She is never left alone without economic support for herself and her children."

Being without a man, without economic support, in a town whose lean economy has only a limited number of jobs for men and even fewer for women is a condition near destitution. Cigar manufacturing offers the most help to a woman without a man and without any other resources. It is a respectable job for a woman; it does not require physical strength nor formal education or extensive training. As a result of these qualifications fourteen of the fifty matriarchs, the largest number employed in any occupation other than "house wife," work in the factories. An unknown number of their adult daughters also find employment in the factories.

However, even with the cigar industry the local economy does not offer much assistance to the mother whose husband has left her. Doña Leonor had sufficient luck with her man that he did not leave her until several of their children were grown. Even so, she has to rely on small amounts of money coming in from a number of sources in order to run her household. Her eldest daughter, who, along with her son, lives with Doña Leonor, works in Chucho's factory and contributes substantially to the upkeep of the house. Ninivé pays for her room and meals, the eldest son periodically returns with money, and Doña herself prepares meals for the occasional transient.

Doña Leonor's explanation for the presence of "true" matriarchy and free union as an alternative to a male dominated, highly Catholic culture may be in part a justification of her own case. Nonetheless, her explanation is also a realistic assessment of what it is to be a female in San Pedro.

Town and Family

Viewed from the institution of the family, the town of San Pedro is a collection of separate social entities, of irreducible social cells, whose outer, protective husk is the house. In contrast with the economic institution, which is a collection of individuals engaged in different occupations, a family is a concrete social group. In contrast with the political and religious institutions, which are social groups but whose diffused membership includes both the President of the Republic and the Pope of the Catholic Church, effective membership in a family stops at the front door. Participation in the economic, political, and religious institutions turns the *sanpedranos* outward, toward other *sanpedranos* and toward people in other communities; participation in the familial institutions turns them inward, toward the intimate world of their wives, husbands, sons, and daughters.

Yet the intimate world of the family does not exist apart from the other institutions or apart from the general setting of the town.

Economically, the *sanpedrano* family is often a complete productive unit, as in the case of farming, or a complete service unit, as in the case of storekeeping. The heads of such families usually take upon themselves to teach their children the ways of their trade just as their fathers had taught them. Politically, the family is the reproductive unit of party loyalty; the affective side of party membership is maintained because it is part of the instruction that children receive from their parents. At least on the local level, the family provides conceptual models for leadership; the actions of the *alcalde* are ostensibly those of a benevolent father guarding his children. In the religious sphere, the family again provides overt conceptual models; the Virgin is like a compassionate mother, Christ-God is a stern father, and the worshippers are innocent children. At the subconscious level, it may be that the mother also provides the emotional content in the model of the suffering Jesus; the image of the long-suffering mother is much closer to that of Jesus than is the image of a mildly rapacious father. Finally, the church and kinship are intricately entangled in the system of *compadrazco*.

The general setting of San Pedro exerts considerable force on the family and on the individual family members. The setting is a product of San Pedro's fusion into Colombian society. This structural articulation into a developing society creates a local environment that rewards mobility, adaptability, and exploitation of opportunities. Seneca represents a person beginning to operate in such an environment. His constant search for a slightly better position, his continual reading of the situation around him, his failure to successfully activate his extended kinship ties, his growing callousness toward similar demands placed on him by his younger brothers, his fear of thieves, his lottery playing are all representative adaptations to an environment heavy with risks and riddled with scarcity. One moral obligation that he fulfills without regard to the social environment is the care that he bestows on his mother. Doña Lola is fortunate that her eldest son carries out this obligation. Without a husband and without a son for financial support, she would be much closer to the brink of absolute destitution.

Loyalty to one's extended kin is difficult to maintain in an environment that maximizes quick mobility and instantaneous exploitation of emphemeral opportunities. The extended system of fictive kinship, *compadrazco*, fairs only slightly better. *Compadrazco* is more capable of expansion than is real kinship. A person's close extended kin are usually in the same economic position as he is, but his *compadre* or his *padrino* may be a wealthy *hacendado*. However, even such an adaptive device as *compadrazco* has trouble functioning effectively in San Pedro.

One specific factor that causes a weakening of extended ties, real or fictive, is population movement. Only 52 percent of the present household heads were born in San Pedro or in nearby Buga or Tuluá. Thus, nearly half of the town's population has lacked behavioral experience in being both godchild and godparent to their present neighbors. If the contemporary movement is an indication of the future, many godchildren, nieces, nephews, and cousins of native *sanpedranos* will move away from the town and never see their godparents, uncles, aunts, and cousins.

The environmental setting of San Pedro is at least in part, responsible for the "true" matriarchal families formed by the extra-legal free union. Free union is a female attempt to reduce the chances of being abandoned, an abandonment, given the scarcity of jobs for women, that will bring economic disaster to the woman and her children.

The environment through which people such as Seneca and Doña Leonor move is one created by the developmental process going on in Colombia. It is an environment of a small town in a developing society.

7

Small Town
in a Developing Society

A S A PLACE, as a human construct on the natural landscape of the Cauca Valley, San Pedro is a geographic constellation of three factors: the institutional activities that its people perform, the cultural tradition that arranges and houses these functions, and the poverty of resources that limits the vigor of its people's performances.

San Pedro is a town because it is a geographic spot upon which are concentrated a number of Colombia's basic institutions. The location of the economic, political, and religious institutions in San Pedro—as well as the educational, medical, and recreational activities—separate it from the smaller *corregimientos*. In turn, the modest performance of these institutions and the relatively few families who participate in them separate San Pedro from the provincial cities of Buga and Tuluá and from the urban complexes of Palmira and Cali.

San Pedro is a *Colombian* town because the arrangement and housing of the institutional activities conforms to a strong, Spanish-American cultural tradition. The tradition is expressed in the dominant theme of perfect rectangularity in plaza, block, and house. The plaza, the architectural and social center of the town, is a place for visiting in the carefully cultivated park, for recreation in the bars and parish hall, for attending to official business in the *alcaldía*, and for worshipping in the church. The block, bounded by a perfect square of intersecting streets, is a continuous front of houses, an uncompromising barrier between street and home activities. The house, the outer husk of the familial cell, is the place for the minimum activities of eating, sleeping, and reproducing, a diminutive fortress against the night's insecurity.

San Pedro is a poor place because it is a town in a developing society, a society that is characterized by a scarcity of resources. San Pedro is also poor because the scarce resources only rarely percolate down to its level; its people do not have sufficient power to bend the flow of resources in their favor. Its poverty is reflected in the incompleteness of its institutions: in the unfinished *alcaldía*, in the minimal distribution of unreliable water, in the equally minimal level of education and medical treatment, and in the undistinguished uniformity of its architecture.

As a people, the *sanpedranos* are Colombian townsmen. As townspeople they are culturally, psychologically, and structurally fused with Colombian society. A comparison of Indian, peasant, and town communities, as painfully inadequate as it must be, will clarify the meaning of cultural, psychological, and structural fusion (Wolf 1959, 1966; Foster 1965).

The culture of a contemporary Indian community in Spanish America has a number of pre-Hispanic traits and even a greater number of Colonial Hispanic configurations. The Indians, including those who speak only Spanish, conceptually close off their world from that of the larger society. Although they may journey out into the alien society to sell and to buy, they shield themselves from contagious contact by wearing "Indian" dress. They call themselves Indians—or some similar name that emphasizes their aberrant ethnicity—and are so referred to by other people. Historical events have pushed them into geographic and social pockets, and their culture is mainly an adaptation to this extreme marginality.

The culture of contemporary peasants is Hispanic, but archaic Hispanic. Many of their ways of speaking, doing, and thinking characterized the Hispanic elite of several centuries past. The rest of their cultural inventory is stocked from their own peasant traditions. They identify with the place where they live rather than with the country of which they are distant citizens. Their structural position is less marginal than that of the Indians, but their participation in the national institutions, particularly in the political one, is extremely limited. Their limited participation is mediated through individuals who stand at the few synaptic points between peasantry and nation and who translate elite culture and power into the local idiom.

The culture of the townsman strives to be as modern as tomorrow and includes items from the non-Hispanic "mass" culture of the United States. The townsman is also known by the place where he lives, but his knowledge of and concern with other places, both Colombian and foreign, is much greater than that of the peasant. His country's institutions ramify throughout his community, and he directly participates in them. Yet he exercises very little control over the institutions of which he is an active part. Unlike the peasant, the townsman is much more sensitive to the fluctuations of the national institutions; like the peasant, he has little control over their direction. His culture is an adaptation to this structural paradox.

San Pedro, being a town, is fused to Colombia through its economic, political, and religious institutions. The performance of economic activities frequently articulates the *sanpedrano* to a national or a regional organization, such as the *Caja Agraria*, the *Junta Comunal*, or the *municipio* offices. The purchase of equipment and the selling of surplus relates him to private individuals in other communities. Sharecroppers, landowning farmers, and cigar makers all try to decrease the risk of a developing economy through diversifying their interest, through being alert for new opportunities, and through denying obligations to extended kin. Despite his efforts and those of his country, the *sanpedrano* cannot extract from the economy the items of *cultura* that his town values demand that he should have. He is disgruntled by his poverty and envious, and suspicious, of those who are not poor. What they have, he wants.

The political roles that the *sanpedrano* plays are those that his country has casted. He is intensely loyal to his political party, but his scorn for politicians reflects his assessment of elite maneuvering and his own lack of political power. He attempts to bypass the impersonal schemes of the *políticos* through creating a personal, long distance tie with a specific national leader. He finds the *alcalde* to be at least an approximation of a power broker who mediates between him and the rapacious powers-that-be. Because his own local self is closely tied with nationhood, his country's failures "pain" him; and *violencia* haunts his comprehension.

As he is a Liberal or a Conservative, the townsman of San Pedro is also a Catholic. Both party and religion are traditional and orthodox. His deviation from the Catholic ideal does not come from Indian survivals or from heresy, but it springs from his apathy toward items that have no relevance to his personal faith. He uses faith to establish an intimate social relation with a specific manifestation of the Catholic supernatural. He sees in Christ a model for the correct way, the godly way, to suffer and to die. With faith, with the Virgin, and with a patiently suffering Christ, the *sanpedrano* is content to ignore and to confuse the remaining ingredients of Catholicism.

As it does in all societies, the family in San Pedro provides primeval models for behavior in non-familial institutions. Beyond the parental models used by the *alcalde* and given to the Virgin and to God, the family responds to, rather than acts on, the setting created by a developing society. The inactive extended kinship ties, the weak *compadrazco* system, and the presence of matriarchal families are eloquent evidence of the impact of the developmental process.

The articulation of its people through the economic, political, and religious institutions to Colombia and the consequential repercussions on the family makes San Pedro more like Mainstreet—Hometown, U.S.A.—than like an Indian or peasant community.

To be sure, there are differences between San Pedro and Mainstreet, differences that reflect the cultural heritage and overall structure of the two nation-states of which the towns are a part. However, the most precise way, although certainly not the most profound way, in which the two towns differ is in the presence or absence of a foreign anthropologist. An Anglo anthropologist has studied San Pedro, but no Colombian anthropologist has studied Mainstreet. The absence of an anthropologist in Mainstreet is not due to the lack of professional Colombian anthropologists. There are Colombian anthropologists whose work ranks with the best of their North American colleagues. Colombian anthropologists, however, study their own country, while North American anthropologists study every country except their own. They scatter about like missionaries and CARE packages in a vaguely unholy and disquieting manner.

One such North American anthropologist, William Sayres, wrote a delightful, warm novel based on his experiences in Colombia. In the book one of the main characters, an anthropologist, said that when he returned to the United States, he was going to write a novel so that he could tell the truth.

This case study is plainly not a novel, but like Sayres, I am struggling to tell the truth. I do not want to predict human behavior. I do not want to draw up scientific laws of human action. I certainly do not want to be a missionary or even a CARE package. I simply want to tell the truth.

How does one tell the truth? I do not know; I am not God. But an anthropological statement is nearing the truth when it begins to lay bare the facts of human existence, when it begins to describe the heroic tragedy of being human.

Humans are like the ancient Mesopotamian hero, Gilgamesh. Gilgamesh, because he was two-thirds god, wanted to see everything, do everything, learn everything, but because he was one-third man, he could not. He was a magnificent creature, who wrestled with the Bull of Heaven sent to destroy him by a jealous goddess; yet despite his strength, when he was near the knowledge of eternal life, he fell asleep; and when he had found a plant that would give man everlasting youth, he was careless and a snake stole it from him.

Seneca, Chucho, and Doña Leonor are like Gilgamesh. They do not wrestle with bulls sent from heaven; they do not go striding across the world searching for eternal life. But as they pursue their destiny within the confines of their small town world, they strive with the same vigor, they feel with the same intensity, they face the same insoluable problem, and they grieve with the same incomprehension as did the hero, Gilgamesh.

This is the truth that Sinclair Lewis described when he wrote *Mainstreet*, and this is the truth about San Pedro.

The truth about San Pedro is in the lives of ordinary townspeople. As they move from doorway to plaza, from making cheap cigars to drinking too much beer, from getting a dirty sludge from their water faucets to watching a third-rate cowboy movie, from exclaiming over the beauty of a used refrigerator to debating the merits of a lottery number, from listening to a soccer game on radio to watching a cow with burning paper on her back, and from proclaiming lasting tranquility to sneering distrustfully, the people of San Pedro are trying to extract an explanation as to the meaning of their existence.

No one knows if they are succeeding.

Recommended Reading

ADAMS, R., 1967, *The Second Sowing: Power and Secondary Development in Latin America*. San Francisco: Chandler Publishing Company.

Analyzes the developmental process without falling into the pit of ethnocentrism.

COHEN, L., 1966, *Colombian Professional Women as Innovators of Culture Change*. Ann Arbor, Mich.: University Microfilms.

A study of the newly emergent group of professional women, a group that is formulating values at variance with those traditionally assigned to them by the elite.

DIX, R., 1967, *Colombia: The Political Dimension*. New Haven, Conn.: Yale University Press.

One of the best of the several recent overall views of Colombia. Recommended for its objectivity.

FALS-BORDA, O., 1955, *Peasant Society in the Colombian Andes*. Gainesville, Fla.: University of Florida Press.

An excellent study of a highland basin community near Bogotá by the foremost Colombian sociologist.

GUZMÁN, G., O. FALS-BORDA, and E. UMAÑA, 1962 and 1964, *La Violencia en Colombia*. Bogotá: Ediciones Tercer Mundo.

A two volume study by Colombians on the "violence," its history and its effect on Colombian society.

INSTITUTO COLOMBIANO DE ANTROPOLOGÍA, *Revista Colombiana de Antropologia*.

Has lengthy articles on both Indian and non-Indian communities.

PAVY, P., 1967, *The Negro in Western Colombia*. Ann Arbor, Mich.: University Microfilms.

A study that is an unusual, fruitful combination of archival and field research on Negroes in Cali and Buenaventura.

POSADA, A. and J., 1966, *The CVC: Challenge to Underdevelopment and Traditionalism*. Bogotá: Ediciones Tercer Mundo.

A comprehensive study of a TVA-like organization that is changing the natural and social landscape of the Cauca Valley. Full of insights that only years of personal observation can give.

REICHEL-DOLMATOFF, G. and A., 1961, *The People of Aritama*. Chicago: University of Chicago Press.

The foremost Colombian anthropologist and his wife have produced an excellent work, rich in details, about a community in the Sierra Nevada de Santa Marta that is undergoing "mestization."

RICHARDSON, M., The Significance of the "Hole" Community in Anthropological Studies. *American Anthropologist*, 69:41–54.

An attempt to grapple with the problem of how to study complex sociocultures through their small communities. See the "Letters to the Editor," *American Anthropologist*, 70:363 for an objection to the use of the word "hole."

SAYRES, W., 1966, *Do Good*. New York: Holt, Rinehart, and Winston Inc.

An insightful, humorous novel about a Peace Corps reject who comes to do good in a Colombian community inhabited by a sexy *curandera* and a skeptical anthropologist.

SCHORR, T., 1965, *Cultural Ecological Aspects of Settlement Patterns and Land Use in the Cauca Valley, Colombia*. Ann Arbor, Mich.: University Microfilms.

A detailed examination of man's use of the Cauca Valley and shows that the large hacienda occupies a functional position in a hierarchy of ecological niches.

SMITH, T., 1967, *Colombia: Social Structure and the Process of Development*. Gainesville, Fla.: University of Florida Press.

A rather ponderous, heavy book by a rural sociologist long familiar with Colombia. The first in a three volume series.

United States Army, 1961, *Area Handbook for Colombia*. Washington, D.C.: U.S. Government Printing Office.

A comprehensive survey with a large bibliography, but the generalizations about social values should be read with several grains of salt.

WILGUS, A. (ed.), 1962, *The Caribbean: Contemporary Colombia*. Gainesville, Fla.: University of Florida Press.

Contains excellent articles by specialists of different fields.

Bibliography

COHEN, L., 1968, Patrones de Prática Profesional en Mujeres. *Educación Médica y Salud*, Vol. 2.

DIX, R., 1967, *Colombia: The Political Dimension*. New Haven, Conn.: Yale University Press.

ERASMUS, C., 1962, Review of *The People of Aritama*. *American Anthropologist*, 64:1105–1106.

FALS-BORDA, O., 1955, *Peasant Society in the Colombian Andes*. Gainesville, Fla.: University of Florida Press.

——, 1957, *El Hombre y la Tierra en Boyacá*. Bogotá: Ediciones Documentos Colombianos.

——, 1964, La Transformación del Agro en Hispanoamérica; El Caso de Nariño en Colombia. *Revista de Ciencias Sociales*, 8:389–402.

FOSTER, G., 1965, Peasant Society and the Image of Limited Good. *American Anthropologist*, 67:293–315.

GUTIÉRREZ DE PINEDA, V., 1958, Alcohol y Cultura en una Clase Obrera, Bogotá. *Homenaje al Profesor Paul Rivet*. Bogotá: Academia Colombiana de Historia.

——, 1962, *La Familia en Colombia*. Bogotá: Centro de Investigaciones Sociales.

HAGEN, E., 1962, *On the Theory of Social Change*. Homewood, Ill.: The Dorsey Press.

HAVENS, A., 1966, *Tamesis: Estructura y Cambio*. Bogotái Ediciones Tercer Mundo.

PARSONS, J., 1949, *Antioqueño Colonization in Western Colombia*. Berkeley, Calif.: University of California Press, Ibero-Americana 32.

——, 1967, *Antioquia's Corridor to the Sea*. Berkeley, Calif.: University of California Press, Ibero-Americana 49.

REICHEL-DOLMATOFF, G., 1960, Notas Etnográficas sobre Los Indios del Chocó. *Revista Colombiana de Antropología*, 9:73–158.

——, and A., 1961, *The People of Aritama*. Chicago: University of Chicago Press.

SMITH, T., 1966, Racial Composition of the Population of Colombia. *Journal of Inter-American Studies*, 7:213–235.

STODDART, D. and TRUBSHAW, J., 1962, Colonization in Action in Eastern Colombia. *Geography*, 47:47–53.

TINNERMEIER, R., 1964, *New Land Settlement in the Eastern Lowlands of Colombia*. Research Paper, No. 13, Madison, Wis.: University of Wisconsin Land Tenure Center.

TORRES RESTREPO, C., 1961, *La Proletarización de Bogotá*. Monografías Sociológicas No. 9. Bogotá: Universidad Nacional de Colombia.

WEST, R., 1957, *The Pacific Lowlands of Colombia*. Baton Rouge, La.: Louisiana State University Press.

——, 1962, The Geography of Colombia. In *The Caribbean: Contemporary Colombia*, ed. A. Wilgus. Gainesville, Fla.: University of Florida Press.

WHITEFORD, A., 1964, *Two Cities of Latin America*. Garden City, N. Y. Doubleday.

WOLF, E., 1959, *Sons of the Shaking Earth*. Chicago: University of Chicago Press.

——, 1966, *Peasants*. Englewood Cliff, N. J.: Prentice Hall.